Mathematics
An Instrument for Living Teaching

by
Richele Baburina

Excerpts from Charlotte Mason's books are accompanied by a reference to which book in the series they came from.
   Vol. 1: Home Education
   Vol. 2: Parents and Children
   Vol. 3: School Education
   Vol. 4: Ourselves
   Vol. 5: Formation of Character
   Vol. 6: A Philosophy of Education

Mathematics: An Instrument for Living Teaching
© 2012, Richele Baburina

All rights reserved. No part of this work may be reproduced or distributed in any form by any means—graphic, electronic, or mechanical, including photocopying, recording, taping, or storing in information storage and retrieval systems—without written permission from the publisher.

ISBN 978-1-61634-201-2 printed
ISBN 978-1-61634-202-9 electronic download

Cover Photo: Oleg Baburin
Cover Design: John Shafer

Published by
Simply Charlotte Mason, LLC
P.O. Box 892
Grayson, Georgia 30017-0892

SimplyCharlotteMason.com

Contents

Mathematics, An Instrument for Living Teaching. 5
Introduction. 7

Part 1: The Importance of Mathematics
Chapter 1: Importance and Educative Value. 11

Part 2: The Teaching of Mathematics
Charlotte Mason Math Grade by Grade. 19
Chapter 2: Arithmetic. 21
Chapter 3: Manipulatives. 49
Chapter 4: Mental Arithmetic and Oral Work 57
Chapter 5: Geography. 67
Chapter 6: Geometry. 73
Chapter 7: Algebra. 85

Appendix
Living Math Books. 93
Choosing a Homeschool Math Curriculum or Textbook 95
Charlotte Mason's Math Timetables by Form. 97
Variations on Scope and Sequence for Form I. 98

Mathematics,
An Instrument for Living Teaching

"I need not touch upon the subject of Mathematics. It is receiving ample attention, and is rapidly becoming *an instrument for living teaching* in our schools" (Vol. 3, p. 236).

Introduction

In my reading of Charlotte Mason's Original Homeschooling Series, I noticed Charlotte used words I had never applied to the study of mathematics—words like joy, beauty, truth, and awe. Disturbingly, Charlotte also seemed to be describing my son, who was "becom[ing] a good arithmetician, applying rules aptly, without seeing the reason of them," although at the time we were using a math curriculum touted as "CM-friendly."

Thus, as a student of Charlotte's philosophy of education and as a mom wanting what is best for her children, this handbook was born. My hope is that you will meet both the profound and the practical in these pages, that any mystery or misunderstanding surrounding Charlotte's thoughts on the study of mathematics will be cleared, and that you will gain assurance in applying Charlotte's methods, whether teaching mathematics yourself or choosing a textbook or curriculum.

Of course, my highest hope is for our children, that they would experience the joy, beauty, truth, and awe found in mathematics. As born persons, they are not empty sacks just waiting to be filled with any number of subjects, even one as worthy as mathematics, but have come into the world with "many relations waiting to be established." Accordingly, this handbook is intended to be a ready reference—a place where you will find Charlotte's methods, words, and ideas gathered together for your convenience—and is not meant to take the place of her complete writings.

May mathematics become an instrument of living teaching in your home!

In His service,
Richele

Part 1

The Importance of Mathematics

Chapter 1
Importance and Educative Value

"How are plans coming for Anna's first year?" Jeanne asked as she poured her friend Erin a glass of iced tea at the kitchen island.

Taking her organizer out of her bag, Erin smiled in reply, "I don't know which of us is more excited. Using living books to impart ideas is what drew me to Charlotte Mason's method of education, and I've chosen *Heidi* as our literature selection for Term One. It was my absolute favorite when I was a girl and I dreamt of reading it with my children even before I became a mother." Erin's smile began to fade, "Math on the other hand is another story. I've read reviews of the CM-friendly math curricula but they all look so different, and math never was my strongest subject . . ."

Sensing the fear creeping into her friend's voice, Jeanne sat down and smiled in encouragement. "What if I told you that math has a lot in common with *Heidi*, your treasured book from childhood?"

"What could math possibly have to do with my little Swiss heroine?" Erin asked, looking doubtful but intrigued.

Jeanne continued, "Do you remember how Heidi passed her days in the sunshine and fresh air of the mountains? Climbing to the high meadows with her friend, Peter, they frolicked among the birds, flowers, and animals, where Heidi grew so strong and healthy that 'nothing could ail her.' Well, Charlotte Mason called mathematics a mountainous land, every bit as vigorous, delightful, and health-giving to the climber as the Swiss Alps were to Heidi. Just as you were excited to learn how great literature breathes life into subjects like history and science, I believe the more you know of Charlotte's ideas surrounding mathematics, the more you will enjoy the same mountain perspective."

Charlotte's Thoughts on the Importance and Educative Value of Mathematics

Habit Training

1. Though the practical value of arithmetic in daily life was not discounted by Charlotte, a higher value was placed on the study of arithmetic for its direct use in the training of both mental and moral habits.

"The practical value of arithmetic to persons in every class of life goes without remark. But the use of the study in practical life is the least of its uses. The chief value of arithmetic, like that of the higher mathematics, lies in the training it

Importance of Mathematics

Notes

See also Volume 2, pages 230 and 231.

The mathematician referred to may have been Maria Agnesi, known for her contributions in calculus as well as her devotion to God and efforts to help the poor and sick. Occasionally staying up late to work on a particular math problem, she would go to bed leaving the problem unsolved only to find the solution written in her own handwriting the next morning. Maria Agnesi lived from 1718 to 1799 in Milan, Italy.

affords to the reasoning powers, and in the habits of insight, readiness, accuracy, intellectual truthfulness it engenders" (Vol. 1, p. 254).

"We divest ourselves of the notion that to develop the faculties is the chief thing, and a 'subject' which does not rise out of some great thought of life we usually reject as not nourishing, not fruitful; while we retain those studies which give exercise in habits of clear and orderly thinking. Mathematics, grammar, logic, etc., are not purely disciplinary, they do develop (if a bull may be allowed) intellectual muscle. We by no means reject the familiar staples of education in the school sense, but we prize them even more for the record of intellectual habits they leave in the brain tissue, than for their distinct value in developing certain 'faculties' " (Vol. 3, p. 174).

"Some Intellectual Habits.— …*Accuracy*, which is to be taught, not only through arithmetic, but through all the small statements, messages, and affairs of daily life" (Vol. 3, p. 120).

"Another realm open to Intellect has an uninviting name, and travelling therein is difficult, what with steep faces of rock to climb and deep ravines to cross. The Principality of Mathematics is a mountainous land, but the air is very fine and health-giving, though some people find it too rare for their breathing. It differs from most mountainous countries in this, that you cannot lose your way, and that every step taken is on firm ground. People who seek their work or play in this principality find themselves braced by effort and satisfied with truth. Intellect now and then calls for the aid of Imagination as he travels here, but not often. My Lord Attorney-General Reason is his chosen comrade" (Vol. 4, Book 1, p. 38).

"Also, there is great joy in standing by, as it were, and watching our own thought work out an intricate problem. There is on record a case of a mathematician who had gone to bed perplexed by a problem, with pencil and paper beside him. He slept, as he believed, soundly all through the night; but, behold, beside him when he awoke, was the problem worked out in the clearest way. He must have done it [*sic*] his sleep" (Vol. 4, Book 1, p. 63).

2. By means of Charlotte's methods—including carefully graduated lessons, daily mental effort, and short word problems within the child's understanding—arithmetic becomes a means of training intellectual and moral habits. In contrast, careless, slipshod teaching, offering crutches, and failing to pronounce sums wrong fosters habits of carelessness in the child.

"Carefully graduated teaching and *daily* mental effort on the child's part at this early stage may be the means of developing real mathematical power, and will certainly promote the habits of concentration and effort of mind" (Vol. 1, p. 257).

"The practical value of arithmetic to persons in every class of life goes without remark. But the use of the study in practical life is the least of its uses. The chief value of arithmetic, like that of the higher mathematics, lies in the training it affords to the reasoning powers, and in the habits of insight, readiness, accuracy, intellectual truthfulness it engenders. There is no one subject in which good teaching effects more, as there is none in which slovenly teaching has more mischievous results. Multiplication does not produce the 'right answer,' so the boy tries division; that again fails, but subtraction may get him out of the bog. There is no *must be* to him; he does not see that one process, and one process *only*, can give the required result. Now, a child who does not know what rule to apply to a simple problem within his grasp, has been ill taught from the first, although he may produce slatefuls of quite right sums in multiplication or long division" (Vol. 1, p. 254).

"Arithmetic is valuable as a means of training children in habits of strict accuracy, but the ingenuity which makes this exact science tend to foster slipshod habits of mind, a disregard of truth and common honesty, is worthy of admiration! The copying, prompting, telling, helping over difficulties, working with an eye to the answer which he knows, that are allowed in the arithmetic lesson, under an inferior teacher, are enough to vitiate any child; and quite as bad as these is the habit of allowing that a sum is *nearly* right, two figures wrong, and so on, and letting the child work it over again. Pronounce a sum *wrong*, or right—it cannot be something between the two. That which is *wrong* must remain *wrong*: the child must not be let run away with the notion that wrong can be mended into right. The future is before him: he may get the next sum right, and the wise teacher will make it her business to see that he *does*, and that he starts with new hope. But the wrong sum must just be let alone" (Vol. 1, pp. 260, 261).

"Therefore his progress must be carefully graduated; but there is no subject in which the teacher has a more delightful consciousness of drawing out from day to day new power in the child. Do not offer him a crutch: it is in his own power he must go" (Vol. 1, p. 261).

"Give him short sums, in words rather than in figures, and excite in him the enthusiasm which produces concentrated attention and rapid work" (Vol. 1, p. 261).

"Let his arithmetic lesson be to the child a daily exercise in clear thinking and rapid, careful execution, and his mental growth will be as obvious as the sprouting of seedlings in the spring" (Vol. 1, p. 261).

Some Habits Developed by the Study of Mathematics Referred to in Charlotte's Writings

Intellectual Habits
Insight
Readiness
Accuracy
Imagining
Intellectual truthfulness
Attention
Concentration
Rapid work
Clear thinking
Careful execution

Notes

John Ruskin was a prominent nineteenth-century writer, art teacher, and critic, as well as a renowned social and educational reformer in England.

Euclid, fl. 300 B.C., was an Alexandrian Greek mathematician often referred to as the "Father of Geometry." Euclid often used proof by contradiction or reductio ad absurdum. *Simply put, when wishing to prove something true, it is assumed not true in order to show that the consequences of this leads to an absurd conclusion.*

"This is what the LORD says: 'If I have not made my covenant with day and night and established the fixed laws of heaven and earth, then I will reject the descendants of Jacob and David my servant' " (Jeremiah 33:25, 26, NIV).

Ordered Thinking
Effort
Effort of mind
Neatness
Deftness

Moral Habits
Truthfulness
Honesty

Beauty and Truth

3. Charlotte's philosophy of education does not allow separation between the intellectual and spiritual life of children. Accordingly, it is the beauty and truth of mathematics—that awakening of a sense of awe in God's fixed laws of the universe—which allows the study of mathematics its rightful place in the curriculum.

"Never are the operations of Reason more delightful and more perfect than in mathematics. Here men do not begin to reason with a notion which causes them to lean to this side or to that. By degrees, absolute truth unfolds itself. We are so made that truth, absolute and certain truth, is a perfect joy to us; and that is the joy that mathematics afford" (Vol. 4, Book 1, pp. 62, 63).

"If the use of words be a law unto itself, how much more so the language of figures and lines! We remember how instructive and impressive Ruskin is on the thesis that 'two and two make four' and cannot by any possibility that the universe affords be made to make five or three. From this point of view, of immutable law, children should approach Mathematics; they should see how impressive is Euclid's 'Which is absurd,' just as absurd as would be the statements of a man who said that his apples always fell upwards, and for the same reason. The behaviour of figures and lines is like the fall of an apple, fixed by immutable laws, and it is a great thing to begin to see these laws even in their lowliest application. The child whose approaches to Arithmetic are so many discoveries of the laws which regulate number will not divide fifteen pence among five people and give them each sixpence or ninepence; 'which is absurd' will convict him, and in time he will perceive that 'answers' are not purely arbitrary but are to be come at by a little boy's reason" (Vol. 6, p. 152).

"The question of Arithmetic and of Mathematics generally is one of great import to us as educators. So long as the idea of 'faculties' obtained no doubt we were right to put all possible weight on a subject so well adapted to train the reasoning powers, but now we are assured that these powers do not wait upon our training. They are there in any case; and if we keep a chief place in our curriculum for Arithmetic we must justify ourselves upon other grounds. We take strong ground when we appeal to the beauty and truth of Mathematics; that, as Ruskin points out, two and two make four and cannot conceivably make five, is an inevitable law. It is a great thing to be brought into the presence of a law, of a whole system of laws, that exist without our concurrence,—that two straight lines cannot enclose a space is a fact which we can perceive, state, and act upon but cannot in any wise alter, should give to children the sense of limitation which is wholesome for all of us, and inspire that *sursum corda* which we should hear in all natural law" (Vol. 6, pp. 230, 231).

"By degrees children get that knowledge of God which is the object of the final daily prayer in our beautiful liturgy—the prayer of St. Chrysostom—'Grant us in this world knowledge of Thy truth,' and all other knowledge which they obtain gathers round and illuminates this" (Vol. 6, p. 64).

"Where science does not teach a child to wonder and admire it has perhaps no educative value" (Vol. 6, p. 224).

4. Good teachers take the time to introduce the inspiring ideas and living truths found in mathematics while also being careful not to cloud their teaching with excessive explanations.

"Mathematics depend upon the teacher rather than upon the text-book and few subjects are worse taught; chiefly because teachers have seldom time to give the inspiring ideas, what Coleridge calls, the 'Captain' ideas, which should quicken imagination" (Vol. 6, p. 233).

"I have said much of history and science, but mathematics, a mountainous land which pays the climber, makes its appeal to mind, and good teachers know that they may not drown their teaching in verbiage" (Vol. 6, p. 51).

Proportion in Curriculum

5. The study of mathematics is necessary but should not be given undue importance, especially at the expense of a full and generous curriculum.

"Mathematics are delightful to the mind of man which revels in the perception of law, which may even go forth guessing at a new law until it discover that law; but not every boy can be a champion prize-fighter, nor can every boy 'stand up' to Mathematics. Therefore perhaps the business of teachers is to open as many doors as possible in the belief that Mathematics is one out of many studies which make for education, a study by no means accessible to everyone. Therefore it should not monopolise undue time, nor should persons be hindered from useful careers by the fact that they show no great proficiency in studies which are in favour with examiners, no doubt, because solutions are final, and work can be adjudged without the tiresome hesitancy and fear of being unjust which beset the examiners' path in other studies" (Vol. 6, pp. 152, 153).

"We would send forth children informed by 'the reason firm, the temperate will, endurance, foresight, strength and skill,' but we must add resolution to our good intentions and may not expect to produce a reasonable soul of fine polish from the steady friction, say, of mathematical studies only" (Vol. 6, p. 153).

"Again, integrity in our dealings depends largely upon 'Mr. Micawber's' golden rule, while 'Harold Skimpole's' disregard of these things is a moral offence against

Notes

Sursum corda is Latin for "Lift up your hearts," an invitation found in Christian liturgy to lift one's heart to God.

Excerpt from "She Was a Phantom of Delight" by English poet William Wordsworth (1770–1850).

Notes

Wilkins Micawber is a fictional character from Charles Dickens' 1850 novel, David Copperfield, *who, though poor, always remained optimistic. Micawber's golden rule of living within one's means is based upon his experience that "Annual income twenty pounds, annual expenditure nineteen and six [i.e., six pence less than twenty pounds], result happiness. Annual income twenty pounds, annual expenditure twenty pounds ought six [i.e., six pence more than twenty pounds], result misery."*

Harold Skimpole was a major character in Charles' Dickens' novel, Bleak House. *Known as an irresponsible idler, he had neither the desire nor the ability to conduct financial or business transactions. Feigning naivete he sponged off his friends and was bent on enjoying life rather than facing any of its challenges. Using Dickens' well-known characters, Charlotte showed the great worth of mathematics outside of those reasons most commonly given for its study.*

The French phrase bête noire *translates literally to "black beast" and is used figuratively to describe an idea or person that is abhorred and to be avoided.*

For more of Charlotte's thoughts on children's gifts, see chapter 8 of Parents and Children, *Volume 2.*

society. Once again, though we do not live on gymnastics, the mind like the body, is invigorated by regular spells of hard exercise" (Vol. 6, p. 231).

"But education should be a science of proportion, and any one subject that assumes undue importance does so at the expense of other subjects which a child's mind should deal with. Arithmetic, Mathematics, are exceedingly easy to examine upon and so long as education is regulated by examinations so long shall we have teaching, directed not to awaken a sense of awe in contemplating a self-existing science, but rather to secure exactness and ingenuity in the treatment of problems" (Vol. 6, p. 231).

"In a word our point is that Mathematics are to be studied for their own sake and not as they make for general intelligence and grasp of mind. But then how profoundly worthy are these subjects of study for their own sake, to say nothing of other great branches of knowledge to which they are ancillary! Lack of proportion should be our *bête noire* in drawing up a curriculum, remembering that the mathematician who knows little of the history of his own country or that of any other, is sparsely educated at the best" (Vol. 6, p. 232).

"At the same time Genius has her own rights. The born mathematician must be allowed full scope even to the omission of much else that he should know. He soon asserts himself, sees into the intricacies of a problem with half an eye, and should have scope. He would prefer not to have much teaching" (Vol. 6, p. 232).

"To sum up, Mathematics are a necessary part of every man's education; they must be taught by those who know; but they may not engross the time and attention of the scholar in such wise as to shut out any of the score of 'subjects,' a knowledge of which is his natural right" (Vol. 6, p, 233).

"First and chiefest is the knowledge of God, to be got at most directly through the Bible; then comes the knowledge of man, to be got through history, literature, art, civics, ethics, biography, the drama, and languages; and lastly, so much knowledge of the universe as shall explain to some extent the phenomena we are familiar with and give a naming acquaintance at any rate with birds and flowers, stars and stones; nor can this knowledge of the universe be carried far in any direction without the ordering of mathematics" (Vol. 6, p. 254).

Questions to Ask about the Importance of Mathematics

- Do I recognize the value of mathematics in the training of good habits?
- Am I sure to pronounce sums wrong?
- Am I offering crutches to my child through continual prompting, telling, and helping over difficulties in the arithmetic lessons?
- Do I recognize that there is both beauty and truth in mathematics?
- Do I place either too little or not enough importance on the study of mathematics?
- Am I sure to give the study of mathematics its rightful place in our curriculum?
- Do I allow my gifted child a wider scope in the study of mathematics?

Part 2

The Teaching of Mathematics

Charlotte Mason Math Grade by Grade

The chart below outlines which branches of mathematics were included in Charlotte Mason's curriculum at each grade level. Specifics will be detailed in the chapters ahead.

	Form I			Form II			Forms III & IV			Forms V & VI		
	IB	IA		IIB	IIA							
Approximate U.S. Grade	1	2	3	4	5	6	7	8	9	10	11	12
Approximate U.S. Age	6-7	7-8	8-9	9-10	10-11	11-12	12-13	13-14	14-15	15-16	16-17	17-18
	Elementary Arithmetic			Arithmetic								
	Elementary Geography/ Out-of-Door Geography				Practical Geometry		Geometry					
	Paper Sloyd						Introduction to Elementary Algebra		Algebra			

Chapter 2
Arithmetic

Melissa walked happily into her sunroom. It was spring and the blue coneflowers had recently sprouted. As the tender green leaves smiled at her from their warm, brown bed, her thoughts turned to her son's growth in mathematics this year.

Just as she and her family had looked at the glorious variety of seeds available to them at the nursery, Melissa had gone through Charlotte Mason's writings to discover what needed planting in the windowsill of her child's mind. It was amazing to see what could grow with patience and carefully graduated lessons. Like the unfurling of a seedling, Melissa had noticed her son's development of understanding, concentration, and accuracy.

Flower seeds cannot merely be scattered on top of the soil, Melissa mused, *they must be planted to the correct depth and placed in a warm, well-lit space in order to grow. Likewise, the way in which I teach math is crucial. Short math lessons with interesting oral problems are so motivating. Using manipulatives to convey ideas really helps my son grasp mathematical principles and formulate rules himself.* She shook her head in wonder—her son actually understood the common sense of memorizing multiplication tables, so worked at them with enthusiasm.

As Melissa took care to water her seeds often, so she made sure her son put forth daily mental effort with small, interesting problems. She knew that her tender seedlings could not be transplanted until they had grown at least two "true leaves." Similarly, Melissa needed to be content to go slowly with her son, not moving on to a new rule until he had truly grasped the idea of the first and felt at home working problems with it.

Looking around the sunroom, Melissa was so happy they had taken the time to start seedlings inside; doing so would ensure stronger plants, and she looked forward to the bloom of blue coneflower that would line their walkway this summer. In the same way, having taken the time to put Charlotte Mason's methods into practice, Melissa was preparing the soil for true mathematical thinking and intellectual development in her son.

Arithmetic in Charlotte's Schools

We've seen that Charlotte valued the study of arithmetic primarily for its use in the training of both intellectual and moral habits. Though its use in daily life and business was important, it was the "beauty and truth" of mathematics—that awakening of a sense of awe in God's fixed laws of the universe—that afforded its study a rightful place in Charlotte's curriculum. Now let's take a look at *how* arithmetic was taught in Charlotte's schools because without living teaching, that sense of wonder would not be awakened nor would the desired habit training take place.

Elementary arithmetic spanned the first four school years and was characterized by thorough, careful work in which the children made discoveries for themselves. Grades 1–3 had daily lessons in "Number": five 20-minute lessons and one

Charlotte's students were in school six days per week. See the chart on page 97 for a timetable.

Notes

Information compiled from PNEU Programmes and Examinations, http://www.amblesideonline.org/library.shtml#pneuprogrammes and Charlotte Mason Digital Collection, http://www.redeemer.ca/charlotte-mason.

Quotes cited Stephens refer to Stephens, Irene. "The Teaching of Mathematics to Young Children. The Teaching of Mathematics in the United Kingdom Being a Series of Papers Prepared for the International Commission on the Teaching of Mathematics." London: Wyman & Sons, 1911. No. 11, pp. A2-19. Print. Gutman Library Special Collections.

In 1911, Miss Irene Stephens, a resident of Madras, India, was a guest lecturer in Mathematics at Ambleside. During this visit her paper, "The Teaching of Mathematics to Young Children," was published. Available for purchase in the PNEU office in booklet form, it was used by teachers in both Forms I and II. The paper was also included as a special report in The Teaching of Mathematics in the United Kingdom by the Board of Education (Wyman & Sons, London).

10-minute lesson per week, including rapid mental work for the first year and grades 2 and 3 being exercised on tables (e.g., the multiplication table) for 5-minutes daily.

In fourth grade the five arithmetic lessons increased to 30-minutes in length, including five minutes of mental math. Grades 5 and 6 had only four 30-minute lessons in arithmetic per week with daily mental math, as practical geometry was added to their study. With the addition of formal geometry to the schedule, grades 7 and 8 had three 30-minute arithmetic lessons and three 10-minute sessions of mental arithmetic each week. Grades 9–12 had two 30-minute lessons in arithmetic weekly in which they studied business math, such as profit and loss and simple and compound interest.

The study of junior and senior level arithmetic did not mean a departure from Charlotte's methods. Constant oral practice was given and when sums were written, careful arrangement and neatness was required. Lessons remained carefully graduated; interesting problems of a realistic nature were given with long, tedious calculations omitted.

Elementary Arithmetic

1. Charlotte did not urge any special training or preparation for mathematics in the early years of childhood other than that which occurs in a natural way. The deliberate teaching of elementary arithmetic began in the classroom no earlier than age six.

"I do not think that any direct preparation for mathematics is desirable. The child, who has been allowed to think and not compelled to cram, hails the new study with delight when the due time for it arrives" (Vol. 1, p. 264).

"Taking as our working definition that 'education is an atmosphere, a discipline, a life,' it follows that we realize that education must surround and be a part of the child from his infancy; but until he is ready for school at the end of his sixth year it is to be an education by means of his senses, of his unstudied games, by means of his natural and not of an artificially prepared environment.

"The conscious teaching then of number, as of other definite lines of thought, is to be begun in the schoolroom with a pupil whose age is not less than six years" (Stephens, 1911, p. A2).

2. Elementary Arithmetic in Form I, our approximate grades 1–3, was known as Numbers *or* Sums, *referring to the thorough analysis of numbers presented in a measured, deliberate way.*

"Therefore his progress must be carefully graduated; but there is no subject in which the teacher has a more delightful consciousness of drawing out from day to day new power in the child. Do not offer him a crutch: it is in his own power he must go. Give him short sums, in words rather than in figures, and excite in him the enthusiasm which produces concentrated attention and rapid work. Let his arithmetic lesson be to the child a daily exercise in clear thinking and rapid, careful execution, and his mental growth will be as obvious as the sprouting of seedlings in the spring" (Vol. 1, p. 261).

"Nothing can be more delightful than the careful analysis of numbers and the beautiful graduation of the work, 'only one difficulty at a time being presented to the mind' " (Vol. 1, p. 262).

3. **Numbers** *followed Charlotte's basic principles of short lessons with concentrated attention. The lessons, which were twenty minutes in length, were taught daily. To ensure adequate rest for the child's mind after the required mental effort, an easier lesson followed in the daily schedule.*

"We insist also upon concentration of thought throughout the lessons which range in duration from 20 minutes at first to 25 minutes in the last year; during that time attention and concentrated thinking are required; the children generally have an easy lesson, such as handicrafts or writing, to follow so that their brains are rested after the effort expended" (Stephens, 1911, p. 18).

4. Elementary Arithmetic begins with the concrete—that is, the manipulation of real objects—with the child progressing to the imagining of objects and mental operations using real-world problems before advancing to pure number and written sums.

"A bag of beans, counters, or buttons should be used in all the early arithmetic lessons, and the child should be able to work with these freely, and even to add, subtract, multiply, and divide mentally, without the aid of buttons or beans, before he is set to 'do sums' on his slate" (Vol. 1, p. 256).

"To every teacher of this subject it is now clear that the historical presentation of the subject is the easiest and most natural, *i.e.*, that it is to be presented to the child as it presented itself to the race; beginning with the concrete and working back to the abstract generalisation; and having as far as possible a practical bearing on matters of everyday life" (Stephens, 1911, p. 18).

5. Lessons in **Numbers** *are begun with the thorough exploration of the numbers* one *through* nine, *hallmarked in a Charlotte Mason education by the unfolding of ideas in the child's mind.*

"We generally find that the children, when they enter school, are able to count, but know nothing of the properties of numbers" (Stephens, 1911, p. A2).

"The number one is taken during the first lesson; the children point out to the teacher one window, one fireplace, one piano; in fact, everything in the room which exists singly; then the symbol for one is learnt. Whenever we see a stroke 1 we know that it stands for one of something. The children pick out the ones from groups of figures, and finally learn to write one; getting it as straight and perfect as possible" (Stephens, 1911, p. A2).

"The next number to one is two, as the child probably knows; he learns then to write '2,' first on his board, and then in his book; picks out 2 from a group of figures, and does little sums involving the number 2. Three is taken in the same

Notes

Numbers *refers to the analysis of numbers in the teaching of elementary arithmetic; i.e., the child's investigation of each number by working out addition and subtraction sums involving its use. In Charlotte's lessons, this was initially done with the aid of manipulatives, proceeding to oral or mental work with the writing of sums used very sparingly.*

Charlotte's timetables from 1891 and 1908 both have Swedish Drill, Dancing, or Sol-fa (a singing technique) immediately following the Numbers lessons.

For a thorough exploration of math manipulatives as an aid in Mason's philosophy of education, please refer to chapter 3, "Manipulatives."

Notes

way; and then four, which the pupil must realise is made up of two twos, or of 3 and 1, by very simple little problems such as will readily suggest themselves to any teacher. He learns to count up to 4, and backwards from 4; thus realising slowly the idea of a series of symbols denoting a series of quantities whose magnitudes continue to grow greater. The idea of an *order* of things, which is conveyed by a number, is perhaps grasped most easily by counting a series of things; and that of the relative magnitudes represented by numbers by the little sums in addition and subtraction" (Stephens, 1911, pp. A2–2).

6. Problems within the child's grasp are given.

"Engage the child upon little problems within his comprehension from the first, rather than upon set sums" (Vol. 1, p. 254).

7. As the numbers that the child works with grow larger, the combinations grow more plentiful and a natural overlap with the operations of subtraction and multiplication occurs.

"In this way all the numbers from one to nine are learnt, the examples becoming more numerous as the numbers grow larger, and involving, besides simple subtraction, simple factors such as two threes make six, and three threes make nine" (Stephens, 1911, p. 2).

8. Again, the first lessons are worked with the aid of manipulatives. These are then put away and the subsequent lesson is worked without their use.

"Each number is begun from a concrete set of things, beads, &c., and several questions are asked and answered with the help of the beads. Then these are put away, and for the next lesson work is done on the number without the aid of the concrete" (Stephens, 1911, p. 2).

9. Writing of numbers is done on a small blackboard and then in a notebook with grids.

"The children have a small blackboard and piece of chalk each and on these they first write the numbers; afterwards a book ruled in ¼ inch or ½ inch squares and a lead pencil are requisitioned" (Stephens, 1911, p. 2).

10. The signs +, -, and = are explained after several numbers have been learned.

"When several of the numbers have been learnt the meanings of the signs +, -, and = are explained to the child; + means 'is added to,' or 'is put together with,' – means 'is taken away from,' and = means 'is the same thing as' " (Stephens, 1911, p. 2).

11. Children simultaneously work out addition and subtraction tables by use of the concrete, giving the idea that subtraction is the counterpart to addition.

"He may arrange an addition table with his beans, thus—

0 0   0   = 3 beans

```
0 0    0 0      = 4  "
0 0    0 0 0    = 5  "
```

and be exercised upon it until he can tell, first without counting, and then without looking at the beans, that 2+7=9, etc.

"Thus with 3, 4, 5,—each of the digits: as he learns each line of his addition table, he is exercised upon imaginary objects, '4 apples and 9 apples,' '4 nuts and 6 nuts,' etc.; and lastly, with abstract numbers—6+5, 6+8.

"A subtraction table is worked out simultaneously with the addition table. As he works out each line of additions, he goes over the same ground, only taking away one bean, or two beans, instead of adding, until he is able to answer quite readily, 2 from 7? 2 from 5? After working out each line of addition or subtraction, he may put it on his slate with the proper signs, that is, if he has learned to make figures. It will be found that it requires a much greater mental effort on the child's part to grasp the idea of subtraction than that of addition, and the teacher must be content to go slowly—one finger from four fingers, one nut from three nuts, and so forth, until he knows what he is about" (Vol. 1, pp. 256, 257).

12. Once the signs have been defined, the children will, on occasion, write sums in their books. As a rule, the work is done orally with the writing of sums considered a real treat—to be done only when the children are working well and during the final lesson on a number.

"Now we have the added joy of being able to write sums in our books. This is always considered a privilege, and is only indulged in on mornings when the children are working well, and during the final lesson on some particular number. Writing is still a laborious effort, and is apt to take attention away from the most important matter in hand. The sums are of course always worked orally first, and then written down, *e.g.*, if your little sister is two years old now, how old will she be in two more years? When the answer 4 has been obtained the children write in their books 2+2=4; then they read it; two years added to two years make four years. This writing of sums, however, is very sparingly used, and all the work is oral" (Stephens, 1911, p. 2).

13. The act of writing at this stage still takes great effort and thus should be used sparingly so as not to overshadow the true significance of the lesson.

"Writing is still a laborious effort, and is apt to take attention away from the most important matter in hand" (Stephens, 1911, p. 2).

14. At this stage of learning, and when children are eager and cheerful, simple work with pure number can be attempted with the aim to nurture in them a comfort with numbers.

"During this stage too we give occasional examples dealing with pure number; there are mornings when the little ones are bright and eager, and more than ever anxious to do innumerable sums; this is an opportunity to be seized by the teacher; let us leave the boxes of beads and counters alone, let us even leave out sheep and motor cars, and have nothing but numbers. 'How much left if you take 3 from 5?' 'How much to be added to 4 to make 7?' and so on, quick question and

Notes

In Part V of Volume 1 of the Home Education Series, Charlotte suggests having the child master the "idea of twelve pence in one shilling" before proceeding to units and the ten bundle. Since the decimalization of British currency occurred in 1971, this step can now be demonstrated with ten pence and pennies or a dime and pennies in North America once the number **ten** *has been analyzed.*

	1	
	2	
	3	
	4	
	5	
	6	
	7	
	8	
	9	
1	0	

quick answer, all easy and simple, so that the children may feel at home with the numbers, and feel that they have a real grasp of undoubtedly a function of some minds only, yet it, like an ear for music, can, to a certain extent, be cultivated, to a very limited extent it may be, but even that is worth striving after with our pupils" (Stephens, 1911, p. 2).

15. The number **ten** *is learned in the same way as* **one** *through* **nine**. *Once* **ten** *has been fully analyzed, the terms* **unit** *and* **bundle** *are learned by aid of a variety of manipulatives that can be bundled together in some way.*

"This number we of course learn just as we did the other numbers, *i.e.*, working out addition and subtraction sums involving its use and analysis; then we learn the meaning of the word *unit* and here a few match-sticks seem to serve as the best vehicle to convey the idea we wish to impart. 'When we have 10 things we tie them together and call it a "ten bundle." ' Count out several sets of 10 sticks each and tie them together, now we have several 'ten bundles,' and each of the sticks in a bundle is called a *unit*. Now count out, 1 unit, 2 units, 3 units, 4 units . . . . 9 units, 10 units, and tie them together. This is done several times; and, as one must be careful not to confuse in the child's mind that which is general with that which is particular, let the counting out be done with beads, buttons, pencils, &c., the beads and buttons being threaded in sets of 10 and the pencils, &c., tied together. The name 'ten *bundle*' is used for each of these" (Stephens, 1911, p. 3).

16. Once the children are accustomed to the practice of bundling tens together, writing the number **ten** *and the idea of place value are addressed.*

"When this convention has become habitual to the pupils, it will be time to write the number ten; it is written on the squared paper, one square having 1 written in it for *one* ten bundle, and the next square 0 for 'no units'; now all the other numbers from 1 to 9 are written down under one another, and then 10 is written so that 0 comes under 9, and the 1 is out by itself (to the left) in the 'ten bundle' square" (Stephens, 1911, p. 3).

17. The learning of the numbers 11 through 20 now takes place rapidly using ten bundles and units. The numbers are then counted both forwards and backwards as well as written in columns on grid paper to emphasize place value.

"After 10 is thoroughly mastered the numbers from 11 to 20 are always learnt very quickly as 1 ten bundle and 1 unit; 1 ten bundle and 2 units, &c., &c., use being made of the bundles of matches, threads of beads, &c., though these must be dispensed with as soon as possible. The children practice counting too, both backwards and forwards, and learn to write the numbers in columns so that the idea of the local value of the digits may be impressed upon their minds" (Stephens, 1911, p. 3).

18. At every stage see if the children can tell which new number will come next. This will help ensure they not only have an idea of the number itself but also an idea of where it occurs in relationship to other numbers.

"We try at this stage, and indeed at any stage in the analysis of numbers from 10 to 100, to obtain from the children themselves the composition of each new number that occurs, *e.g.*, we know all numbers from 10 to 13; we have had 10 and no units; 10 and 1 unit, called eleven; 10 and 2 units; 10 and 3 units; then the next number will have to be 10 and 4 units, the next 10 and 5 units, and so on. We find that this sort of counting is necessary, as the children are apt to get an idea of a number by itself, and are unable to realise its position with respect to other numbers" (Stephens, 1911, p. 3).

19. A break in the usual order of lessons is allowed for the introduction of an important teaching aid—money.

"After the number 12 we have to stop for a while, as we are here able to introduce money; for, though it makes a break in the proper sequence of lessons in numbers from 10 to 20, yet it provides such a valuable teaching asset for the future that it is worth the break in the train of thought we have pursued so far" (Stephens, 1911, p. 3).

20. The children receive coin purses containing three different values of coins. After agreeing that carrying lots of pennies would be heavy and take considerable time to count, the children are shown how they could use one coin in place of the pennies.

"We are all provided with purses containing shillings, six-pences, and pennies, and after obtaining from the children the information that lots and lots of pennies would be very heavy to carry about and take a long time to count, we show how instead of six pennies we have a small silver coin and we call it sixpence. Suppose we went into a shop and bought six 1*d.* pieces of chocolate; then instead of counting out six pennies we should just give the shopman *one* coin—one of our sixpences; if we bought 12 penny pieces we might count out 12 pennies (they are counted out by the children), or else we might have,—how many sixpences? (Each set of six pennies is replaced by a 6*d.*); we might have two sixpences, or another coin which we call a shilling and which may be used for two sixpences, or 12 pennies" (Stephens, 1911, pp. 3, 4).

21. Next comes considerable hands-on practice in changing real coins from their coin purses. Children may try experimentally to work with numbers larger than they've already analyzed.

"After this introduction we have practice in changing from pennies to shillings and sixpences, and *vice versa, e.g.* 'count out 18 pennies, we don't want to carry so much, so we change 12 of them into a shilling —count how many are left.'

" 'Six.'

" 'Yes, so that we may have a sixpence instead of those pennies, and we should only take out with us two small coins instead of 18 larger ones.' Or, 'count out 13 pennies, re-place 12 by one shilling, we have one penny over, so that we have two coins instead of 13: count out eight pennies, a sixpence and two pennies,' and so on. As the children deal with numbers larger than 12 the work has to be purely experimental" (Stephens, 1911, p. 4).

22. Numerous money problems that are both simple and of an interesting nature are now given to the children.

"A great many simple sums on money follow the experimental work, the numbers

Notes

Due to the old British currency system, a break occurred at number 12 in order to introduce coins. This natural break will occur at different points based on your monetary system; e.g., at 10 for the introduction of the nickel and dime in North America and five pence and ten pence pieces in the U.K.

20. in U.S. currency—Suppose we went into a shop and bought five 1¢ pieces of candy; then instead of counting out five pennies we should just give the cashier one coin—one of our nickels; if we bought 10 penny pieces we might count out 10 pennies (they are counted out by the children), or else we might have, —how many nickels? (Each set of five pennies is replaced by a nickel); we might have two nickels, or another coin which we call a dime and which may be used for two nickels, or ten pennies.

21. in U.S. currency—'Count out fifteen pennies, we don't want to carry so much, so we change 10 of them into a dime —count how many are left.' 'Five.'

'Yes, so that we may have a nickel instead of those pennies, or we should only take out with us two small coins instead of 15.' Or, 'count out 11 pennies, replace 10 with a dime, we have one penny left over, so that we have two coins instead of 11: count out seven pennies, a nickel and two pennies,' and so on.

Arithmetic

Notes

22. in U.S. currency— The numbers involved should never exceed 10; e.g., I bought three pieces of penny candy, and two gumballs that cost two cents each. I paid the cashier with a dime. How much change did she give me? Or; I found five dimes and gave two cents of each dime to my brother. How much did I give him?

Remember that all these money problems are hands-on exercises.

25. in U.S. currency— Let him have a heap of pennies, say fifty-seven: point out the inconvenience of carrying such weighty money to stores. Lighter money is used—dimes. How many pennies is a dime worth? How many dimes, then, might he have for his fifty-seven pennies? He divides them into heaps of ten, and finds that he has five such heaps. Fifty-seven cents are (or are worth) five dimes and seven pennies. I buy five gumballs at 5¢ apiece; they cost twenty-five cents; show the child how to put down: the pennies, which are worth least, to the right; the dimes, which are worth more, to the left.

At the number 25 the children are introduced to the quarter, and at 50 to the half-dollar or 50-cent-piece.

---

involved never exceeding 12; *e.g.*, I bought three penny balls, two-pennyworth of toffee, and two two-penny balls of string. What change did the shopman give me out of a shilling? Or; I won a prize of *5s.* and gave *2d.* out of every shilling to my brother. How much did I give him?" (Stephens, 1911, p. 4).

23. As new numbers are studied, children continue to work money problems. Since children find these types of problems interesting, they are worked without difficulty.

"We are now able to use money sums to provide us with examples in dealing with all the other numbers; money sums appeal to children, and at this early stage, as well as a little later on, questions involving money appear to be worked very easily" (Stephens, 1911, p. 4).

24. Next, 20 through 100 are taught by means of the ten bundles. The numbers 30 through 100 are taken in groups of ten with repeated practice in counting and notation.

"The number 20 is easily explained as 2 ten bundles, and one finds that the path from 20 to 100 is a smooth one for the child of ordinary intelligence. From 30 onwards the numbers are taken in sets of ten, and frequent practice in counting and in writing the back figures is given" (Stephens, 1911, p. 4).

Notation and Place Value

25. Money and shopping exercises are used as an aid in the vital understanding of notation and place value. As well as changing money, children are taught to place the coins of least value to the right and those worth more to the left.

"When the child is able to work pretty freely with small numbers, a serious difficulty must be faced, upon his thorough mastery of which will depend his apprehension of arithmetic as a science; in other words, will depend the educational value of all the sums he may henceforth do. He must be made to understand our system of notation. Here, as before, it is best to begin with the concrete: let the child get the idea of ten *units* in one *ten* after he has mastered the more easily demonstrable idea of twelve pence in one shilling" (Vol. 1, pp. 257, 258).

"Let him have a heap of pennies, say fifty: point out the inconvenience of carrying such weighty money to shops. Lighter money is used—shillings. How many pennies is a shilling worth? How many shillings, then, might he have for his fifty pennies? He divides them into heaps of twelve, and finds that he has four such heaps, and two pennies over; that is to say, fifty pence are (or are worth) four shillings and twopence. I buy ten pounds of biscuits at fivepence a pound; they cost fifty pence, but the shopman gives me a bill for *4s. 2d.*; show the child how to put down: the pennies, which are worth least, to the right; the shillings, which are worth more, to the left" (Vol. 1, p. 258).

"At the number 20 the children are introduced to the sovereign, and at 24 to the two-shilling piece, and at 30 to the half-crown" (Stephens, 1911, p. 4).

Arithmetic

26. Mastering the ideas of place value and notation is vital, so we need to be content to work slowly and steadily in order to secure the children's understanding in this area. Quicken their minds with the idea that by simple arrangement of only nine numbers and zero, we are able to express all the numbers we could ever name even if we counted all day long for the rest of our lives.

"When the child is able to work freely with shillings and pence, and to understand that 2 in the right-hand column of figures is pence, 2 in the left-hand column, shillings, introduce him to the notion of tens and units, being content to work very gradually. Tell him of uncivilized peoples who can only count so far as five—who say 'five-five beasts in the forest,' 'five-five fish in the river,' when they wish to express an immense number. We can count so far that we might count all day long for years without coming to the end of the numbers we might name; but after all, we have very few numbers to count with, and very few figures to express them by. We have but nine figures and a nought: we take the first figure and the nought to express another number, ten; but after that we must begin again until we get two tens, then, again, till we reach three tens, and so on. We call two tens, twenty, three tens, thirty, because 'ty' (*tig*) means ten.

"But if I see figure 4, how am I to know whether it means four tens or four ones? By a very simple plan. The *tens* have a place of their own; if you see figure 6 in the ten-place, you know it means sixty. The tens are always put behind the units: when you see two figures standing side by side, thus, '55,' the left-hand figure stands for so many tens; that is, the second 5 stands for ten times as many as the first" (Vol. 1, pp. 258, 259).

27. Mastering the idea of tens and units will set the foundation for the children to easily grasp the idea of a hundreds place. Again, no written sums are to be given here, and the children should not work with numbers further than what has been learned in our system of notation. When children do reach the point of "carrying" in addition or multiplication problems, they should say they are "carrying" two tens or three hundreds—not "carrying" two or three, or whatever the case may be.

"Let the child work with tens and units only until he has mastered the idea of the tenfold value of the second figure to the left, and would laugh at the folly of writing 7 in the second column of figures, knowing that thereby it becomes seventy. Then he is ready for the same sort of drill in hundreds, and picks up the new idea readily if the principle have been made clear to him, that each remove to the left means a tenfold increase in the value of a number. Meantime, 'set' him no sums. Let him never work with figures the notation of which is beyond him, and when he comes to 'carry' in an addition or multiplication sum, let him not say he carries 'two,' or 'three,' but 'two tens,' or 'three hundreds,' as the case may be" (Vol. 1, p. 259).

The Four Rules and Tables

Addition and Subtraction

28. The thorough examination of numbers from 1 to 100 occurs in the first

---

Notes

26. in U.S. currency—When the child is working freely with dimes and pennies, and understands that a 2 in the right-hand column of figures is pennies, and a 2 in the left-hand column, dimes, introduce the idea of tens and units, being content to work slowly and steadily.

Rather than use the Victorian term *uncivilized* you may wish to say "remote," "far away," or even "in the past" in its place.

Notes

year of formal education and the four rules and tables are begun in the second year.

"The analysis of numbers from 1 to 100 occupies the first year; with the second year we begin the four rules and tables" (Stephens, 1911, p. 4).

29. Children simultaneously work out addition and subtraction tables by use of the concrete, giving the idea that subtraction is the counterpart to addition.

"He may arrange an addition table with his beans, thus—

0 0   0   = 3 beans

0 0   0 0   = 4 "

0 0   0 0 0   = 5 "

and be exercised upon it until he can tell, first without counting, and then without looking at the beans, that 2+7=9, etc.

"Thus with 3, 4, 5,—each of the digits: as he learns each line of his addition table, he is exercised upon imaginary objects, '4 apples and 9 apples,' '4 nuts and 6 nuts,' etc.; and lastly, with abstract numbers—6+5, 6+8.

"A subtraction table is worked out simultaneously with the addition table. As he works out each line of additions, he goes over the same ground, only taking away one bean, or two beans, instead of adding, until he is able to answer quite readily, 2 from 7? 2 from 5? After working out each line of addition or subtraction, he may put it on his slate with the proper signs, that is, if he has learned to make figures. It will be found that it requires a much greater mental effort on the child's part to grasp the idea of subtraction than that of addition, and the teacher must be content to go slowly—one finger from four fingers, one nut from three nuts, and so forth, until he knows what he is about" (Vol. 1, pp. 256, 257).

30. Small problems with abstract numbers are given, using manipulatives as necessary, but the children are encouraged to work with imaginary beans as a step toward the abstract.

"He will be able to work with promiscuous numbers, as 7+5−3. If he must use beans to get his answer, let him; but encourage him to work with *imaginary* beans, as a step towards working with abstract numbers" (Vol. 1, p. 257).

31. Addition problems dealing with money begin with adding smaller denominations and progressing to larger denominations.

"Here the first sums given are those dealing with money. Addition of pence, *e.g.*, 7*d*. + 4*d*. and then 7*d*. + 6*d*. + 2*d*. is followed by addition of shillings and pence, *e.g.*, 4*s*. 3*d*. + 2*s*. 6*d*. and then 4*s*. 9*d*. + 17*s*. 4*d*., then of pounds, shillings, and pence, the numbers of £ being small: —

```
              £  s.  d.
  e.g.,       9  10  5
              3  17  8
              ─────────
  Answer     13   8  1
```

The abbreviations for pounds, shillings, and pence, £, s. d., come from the Latin words **librae, solidi, denarii.** *Before the decimalization of British currency in 1971, 12 pennies were in a shilling and 20 shillings made a pound.*

8 pennies and 4 pennies make 1 shilling, and leave 1 penny over; 1 shilling and 17 shillings make 18 shillings, which, with 2 shillings, make 1£., and leave 8 shillings over; £1 + £3 + £9 = £13. Our answer is, therefore, £13 8*s.* 1*d.*; and, finally, farthings are introduced" (Stephens, 1911, p. 7).

32. Sums with abstract numbers, referred to as **pure** *numbers, are given with the child paying careful attention to place value.*

"After the children have worked some little time at the addition of money, sums on pure number are given them; *e.g.*, 674 + 215; this is to be written in a new way: —

674
215

the hundreds, tens, and units in their own places. 4 units + 5 units = 9 units, to be written in the units' place. 1 ten + 7 tens = 8 tens, to be written in the tens' place. 2 hundreds + 6 hundreds = 8 hundreds, to be written in the hundreds' place,

"The finished sum is then:—

674
215
889 Answer" (Stephens, 1911, p. 7).

33. The children are taught to add **in tens** *when sums involving "carrying" are introduced.*

"The next step is a sum like: —

519
392

"In a case like this the children are taught to add in tens, *e.g.*, 2 units + 9 units = 10 units and 1 = 11 units, *i.e.*, 1 unit for the units' place and a ten to be added on to the others. 1 ten + 9 tens = 10 tens, or one hundred, and there is still one ten. We therefore have one hundred and one ten; and the one hundred + three hundreds + five hundreds give us nine hundreds:—

519
392
911 Answer" (Stephens, 1911, pp. 7, 8).

34. At this point, longer sums with three or more sets of figures may be given—with the children continuing to add in tens. The changing of units to tens, and tens to hundreds comes naturally to them since they are already familiar with changing money.

"After this longer sums may be given, with three, or four, or more sets of figures,

Notes

31. in U.S. currency— *Addition of pennies, e.g., 7 pennies + 2 pennies and then 7 pennies + 2 pennies + 2 pennies is followed by addition of dimes and pennies, e.g., 4 dimes and 3 pennies + 2 dimes and 6 pennies. And then 4 dimes and 8 pennies + 3 dimes and 3 pennies, then dollars, dimes and pennies, the numbers of $ being small: —*
e.g.,

	$	dimes	pennies
	5.	6	7
+	9.	8	4
Answer	15.	5	1

7 pennies and 3 pennies make one dime, and leave 1 penny over; 8 dimes and 2 dimes make 1 dollar and leave 5 dimes over; 9 dollars and 1 dollar and 5 dollars make 15 dollars. Our answer is, therefore, 15 dollars, 5 dimes and 1 penny or $15.51.

Have children add **in tens** *for accuracy.*

Notes

34. in U.S. currency—i.e., to write the 11 units as one in the units' place and put the ten in with the other tens; and with amounts like 13 pennies, which is one dime and three pennies; or 14 dimes, which is a dollar and forty cents if it is a money question. The changing of units to tens, and tens to hundreds comes naturally to them since they are already familiar with changing pennies into dimes, and dimes into dollars.

35. in U.S. currency—e.g., if a kitten cost $5.00, a collar cost $2.49 and a bag of kitten food cost $3.99, what was the total cost?

36. in U.S. currency—e.g., (a) if I have 10¢ in my pocket and trade my brother 5¢ for a Lego® piece, how much have I left; or (b) if I have six nuts and I want 9, how many more must I get?

37. in U.S. currency—For example, take away 1 dime and 2 pennies from 5 dimes and 8 pennies, and what is left?

```
    dimes  pennies
      5      8
      1      2
      4      6
```

Two pennies and 6 pennies make 8 pennies, and 1 dime + 4 dimes = 5 dimes.

(continued on p. 33)

---

the children always adding in tens and thus attaining a mechanical accuracy. The children are always able after a little judicious questioning to tell us what to do with the 11 units and 11 tens in the sum given above; *i.e.*, to write the 11 units as one in the units' place and put the ten in with the other tens; and with amounts like 13 pennies, which is one shilling and one penny; or 27 shillings, which is a pound and seven shillings, if it were a money question. The analogy between the changing of pennies into shillings, shillings into pounds, and the changing of units into tens, and tens into hundreds, makes the latter seem quite easy and natural to the children" (Stephens, 1911, p. 8).

35. Following these, the children are given thought-provoking problems dealing with either money or abstract numbers.

"Interesting problems to be worked by the addition of money, or of pure numbers come next, *e.g.*, if a bicycle cost £5 0*s*. 0*d*., a tool-case 2*s*. 6 *d*., and a bell 1*s*. 9*d*., and a lamp 5*s*. 6*d*., what was the total cost?" (Stephens, 1911, p. 8).

36. Subtraction is now more formally introduced in the same way as addition, that is, using interesting real-life problems and simple money sums. Examples presenting subtraction as the complement to addition are considered best and should be used more frequently.

"Subtraction is introduced as addition was, by little money sums practically presented at first, *e.g.*, (*a*) if I have 6*d*. in my purse and give a porter 2*d*. for carrying a parcel, how much have I left; or (*b*) If I have six nuts and I want 9, how many more must I get? Examples of the nature of (*b*) are advisable, and should be the more numerous because the children can add more easily than they can subtract; and, also, such examples give them the idea of subtraction as the complement of addition; and this view of subtraction is now generally accepted as the right one to be given to beginners, and is used in later lessons on this part of the work" (Stephens, 1911, p. 8).

37. Next come subtraction sums involving larger values of money and the term "take away" is brought into use. These sums are first worked in the concrete, with children using their coin purses, and then with money problems written in their notebooks.

"After one or two such examples we begin sums involving shillings, and begin to use the term 'take away.' Take away 1*s*. 2*d*. from 5*s*. 8*d*., and what is left?

```
  s.  d.
  5   8
  1   2
  4   6.
```

"Two pennies and 6 pennies make 8 pennies, and 1 shilling + 4 shillings = 5 shillings.

"Next come sums like this: I had 10 shillings and I paid a man 3*s*. 9*d*., what had I left? Just at first this should be done experimentally; the child attempts to pay 3*s*. 9*d*. out of a purse containing 10 shillings and finds the 9*d*. a difficulty for a little while, though it will soon occur to him to change it into pennies. He then works several sums in his book, mentally changing a shilling into pennies, and presently pounds into shillings" (Stephens, 1911, p. 8).

38. Having first become accustomed to changing coins of larger value into those of smaller value, it is relatively simple for the children to change tens into units when subtraction using abstract numbers is begun.

"When we arrive at subtraction sums involving pure number it is a comparatively simple thing to change tens into units after having already become familiar with the changing of pounds into shillings and shillings into pence; *e.g.*, subtract (we have now learnt that this is the same as 'take away') 27 from 41:—

41
<u>27</u>

"We cannot take 7 units from 1 unit—what shall we do? Someone in the class will probably suggest 'Turn a 10 into units.' We now have 11 units, and 7 + 4 units = 11 units. Then we take 2 tens from 3 tens as 1 has been turned into units; and our sum is:—

41
<u>27</u>
<u>14</u> Answer" (Stephens, 1911, p. 9).

39. If this step is not fully understood, the manipulatives are brought out to illustrate how a ten bundle is broken into units.

"If this should not be clear we go back to our bundle of match sticks and break one up into its component units" (Stephens, 1911, p. 9).

40. "Equal Additions" can be taught as an alternate method of two-digit subtraction. This is believed to be a quicker way of working subtraction, so teaching it should be taken into consideration.

"Though it is generally advisable to give a class only one method of subtraction and the 'Decomposition' method just mentioned is the one most easily explained, yet, we may just glance at the method of 'Equal Additions' which some teachers prefer.

"We begin with our bundle of matchsticks. To take 28 from 47, we have before us 4 ten bundles and 7 units—take 8 from 7, we cannot, therefore, instead of untying one of the ten bundles we have, we get a whole new bundle and untie it; we now have 4 tens and 17 units and taking away 8 we have 9 units left. Now we are to take 2 tens away, take them and remember to remove the ten bundle which we put in, *i.e.*, take 3 ten bundles away. This last little 'Rule,' if we may call it so, is arrived at by the pupil after he has worked several examples. The method of equal additions is eventually a more rapid way of working subtraction and is therefore worth attention" (Stephens, 1911, p. 9).

Notes

Then come problems like this: I had ten dimes and I had to pay the cashier 39¢, what had I left? At first this should be done experimentally; the child attempts to pay 3 dimes and 9 pennies out of a coin purse containing 10 dimes and finds the 9¢ a difficulty for a little while, though it will soon occur to him to change it into pennies. He then works several problems in his notebook, mentally changing a dime into pennies, and then dollars into dimes.

38. in U.S. currency—It is relatively simple for the children to change tens into units when subtraction using abstract numbers is begun, having first become accustomed to changing dollars into dimes and dimes into pennies.

The "Decomposition" method in subtraction is also known as "regrouping" and involves breaking a ten bundle into smaller units. This method is also called "borrowing"; i. e., borrowing an amount from a higher place value and giving it to a lower place value. In the "Equal Additions" method equal amounts are added to both numbers, avoiding the need for borrowing (10 units being the value added to the top figure and one ten added to the bottom figure in the sample).

Notes

41. Children now work subtraction problems incorporating everything studied up to this point.

"Problems follow involving subtraction of money and pure number and embodying all that has been learnt so far" (Stephens, 1911, p. 9).

Multiplication and Division

42. Multiplication is introduced as repeated addition through simple, interesting problems. The symbol "×" is explained and children write several examples using small numbers on their blackboards.

"Multiplication is at first presented as an extension of addition, *e.g.*, 'If 4 children had 6*d*. each, how much had they altogether?' would be worked 6*d*. + 6*d*. + 6*d*. + 6*d*. = 24*d*. = 2*s*. Several examples like this are given before we suggest that it may be written down more shortly, thus 6*d*. × 4, where ' × 4' means multiplied by 4, *i.e.*, each of the quantities mentioned is to be taken 4 times, so that 6*d*. × 4 means 4 sixpences, 2*s*. × 10 would mean 10 2*s*. pieces, and so on.

"We work a few simple questions, getting the children to write them on their blackboards with the multiplication sign and using easy numbers for which a knowledge of the multiplication table is not necessary. These elementary examples give to the children an idea of what 'times' indicates and we can then begin Tables" (Stephens, 1911, pp. 9, 10).

42. in U.S. currency—e.g., 'If 4 children had 5¢ each, how much had they altogether?' would be worked 5¢ + 5¢ + 5¢ + 5¢ = 20¢ = 2 dimes. Several examples like this are given before suggesting that it may be written down more shortly, thus 5¢ × 4, where '× 4' means multiplied by 4, i.e., each of the quantities mentioned is to be taken 4 times, so that 5¢ × 4 means four 5¢, 1 dime × 10 would mean ten dimes, etc.

43. Using manipulatives each child constructs a multiplication table, providing a tangible way to grasp its rationale while also reinforcing the idea of multiplication as repeated addition. Understanding the basis of multiplication tables lays the groundwork for future mathematical training.

"The child may learn the multiplication-table and do a subtraction sum without any insight into the *rationale* of either. He may even become a good arithmetician, applying rules aptly, without seeing the reason of them; but arithmetic becomes an elementary mathematical training only in so far as the reason why of every process is clear to the child. 2+2=4, is a self-evident fact, admitting of little demonstration; but 4×7=28 may be proved.

"He has a bag of beans; places four rows with seven beans in a row; adds the rows, thus: 7 and 7 are 14, and 7 are 21, and 7 are 28; how many sevens in 28? 4. Therefore it is right to say 4×7=28; and the child sees that multiplication is only a short way of doing addition" (Vol. 1, pp. 255, 256).

44. Multiplication tables as far as 6×12 are made with the use of concrete objects.

"When the child can add and subtract numbers pretty freely up to twenty, the multiplication and division tables may be worked out with beans, as far as 6×12; that is, 'twice six are 12' will be ascertained by means of two rows of beans, six beans in a row" (Vol. 1, p. 257).

45. With assistance, children also construct the multiplication table in

*written form, giving them another tool to understanding the r[ationale]
behind it.*

"To help the children to see the rationale of the multiplication table, first construct each one for themselves with the teacher's assistance, *e.g.*, s[ay] it were 4 times, the teacher begins 'I write down one 4 on the board with [a] 1 above it, to show how many fours I have. Then I write down another fou[r. How] many have I?' 'Two.' 'How much have I now, two fours that is?' 'Eight.' Pu[t 8] down underneath the second 4. Now write down another four, we have three [fours] or 12, similarly four fours or 16, five fours or 20, and so on to the end of the [table,] 12 fours or 48, until the whole table stands: —

1	2	3	4	5	6	7	8	9	10	11	12
4	4	4	4	4	4	4	4	4	4	4	4
	8	12	16	20	24	28	32	36	40	44	48

(Stephens, 1911, p. 10).

46. Children go through several steps in learning the multiplication table:

1. Form a mental picture by looking at the table intently.
2. Say the table through several times.
3. Several figures in the table are erased for the child to fill in.
4. The table is again written out but with new gaps to be filled in.
5. Repeat the table aloud once more.

"The children look at this for some time, visualising it as an aid to committing it to memory, and then say it through several times. The teacher then rubs out several figures here and there in the table and lets the children fill in the gaps thus left. Then the whole table is written out again with several gaps to be filled in by the pupils. The whole table is then said through again by each one" (Stephens, 1911, p. 10).

47. It is essential that the multiplication table be committed to memory and learned in a variety of ways, not just in consecutive order. If you have more than one child, the table should be learned individually and not only recited in chorus.

"There is no royal road to the multiplication table; it *must* be learnt by heart. This is a fact which faces every teacher of elementary arithmetic, and which each must prepare for in the best way possible. They must be learnt by each child individually and not in a chorus. The tables are learnt both forwards and backwards as it were, *i.e.*:—

6 times 1 = 6.
6 times 2 = 12, &c., and also
One 6 is 6.
Two 6's are 12.
Three 6's are 18 &c., &c., and are said not in consecutive order, but in a variety of ways, *e.g.*—
Four 6's are 24.
Three 6's are 18.
Six 6's are 36.

Seven 6's are 42.
Ten 6's are 60, &c.,
and then again in another order" (Stephens, 1911, p. 10).

48. Each time a table is learnt by heart, problems including its use are given together with review problems from previous tables learnt. The child should be able to tell you how the problem is worked. As always, begin with money problems before progressing to abstract numbers.

"As each table is mastered examples involving its use and that of previous ones are given, always in the nature of problems beginning with money questions as in addition and subtraction, and proceeding to the manipulation of pure number; *e.g.*:— A boy was collecting shells, he got 23 every day for 72 days, how many had he then? The sum is written:—

$$72 \times 23$$
$$\underline{23}$$

and the multiplication is worked by 20 first and 3 afterwards. The information as to how it is to be done is obtained from the child, he is able to tell you that you can do it by multiplying by 20 and 3 and adding the products, and that multiplying by 20 is easy because it is just multiplying by 2 and adding a cipher. The finished sum is:—

$$72 \times 23$$
$$\underline{23}$$
$$1{,}440$$
$$\underline{216}$$
$$\underline{1{,}656} \text{ Answer}$$

(Stephens, 1911, pp. 10, 11).

A cipher is a zero.

49. When writing problems, make sure the child is keeping proper place value alignment.

"Great care is bestowed in seeing that the units, tens, and hundreds are kept in their proper columns all through the sum" (Stephens, 1911, p. 11).

50. Multiplying by hundreds and thousands should be straightforward, with two zeroes added for the hundreds, and three zeroes for the thousands.

"To multiply by hundreds and thousands is also found quite simple when worked in the same way" (Stephens, 1911, p. 11).

51. Division is begun in the concrete as each multiplication table is learned.

"When the child can say readily, without even a glance at his beans, 2x8=16, 2x7=14, etc., he will take 4, 6, 8, 10, 12 beans, and divide them into groups of two: then, how many twos in 10, in 12, in 20? And so on, with each line of the multiplication table that he works out" (Vol. 1, p. 257).

52. Two different meanings of Division need to be communicated—the idea of continuous subtraction or sharing and the idea of fractional parts, also known as measuring.

"We have now two different meanings to convey: the one idea of continuous subtraction, the other an idea of fractional parts" (Stephens, 1911, p. 11).

53. The idea of continuous subtraction is given through "sharing" exercises. Working with manipulatives, children share nuts or candy into heaps. It is then pointed out that this sharing into heaps, or putting into groups, is called division and more problems are worked.

"Now he is ready for more ambitious problems: thus, 'A boy had twice ten apples; how many heaps of 4 could he make?'" (Vol. 1, p. 257).

"The first one can impart by exercises in 'sharing' worked with real nuts or pennies just at first; share 12 nuts out into heaps of three, how many boys must there be if each is to have three nuts, how many if each were to have two? How many sticks of chocolate could you buy if each cost *2d.* and you had *6d.* to spend? This sharing into heaps of 2 or 3, &c., is called division by 2 or 3, &c. Suppose I asked you to divide 15 into threes, what would you do? Divide it into heaps of 3 and we should have 5 heaps because there are 5 threes in 15. If I divide 8 by 2, how many heaps have I? How many if I divide 10 by 5? 18 by 6? &c., &c." (Stephens, 1911, p. 11).

54. Now present the symbol for division, explaining that the symbol means "divided by." Some simple money problems are then worked out.

"The sign ÷ for division is explained, and a few simple money sums worked next, *e.g.,* £6 12*s.* 4*d.* ÷ 2 = £3 6*s.* 2*d.*" (Stephens, 1911, p. 11).

55. Short division is then introduced with problems involving tens. If needed, manipulatives are used to demonstrate the problem.

"After this they learn how to divide when the numbers involve tens, and to write the division as short division, *e.g.,*

2)48
　24　　*e.g.,* two tens and a four;

this is demonstrated with 'ten bundles' if necessary. We have by now discarded our idea of 'heaps' of 2, and realise that 48 ÷ 2 means the number of two's there are in 48. 4 tens ÷ 2 = 2 tens, and 8 ÷ 2 = 4 units; the answer to 48 ÷ 2 is therefore 24" (Stephens, 1911, p. 11).

56. Long Division is presented next, using money problems with a small divisor, breaking the problem down into steps.

"Some children may not be able to do this, but it is worth trying. We begin with money sums, and a small number as divisor, and say that this is a new way of putting down division sums, so that we can *see* the Remainder after dividing into the pounds, shillings, and pence; or hundreds, tens and units, *e.g.,*

4)924(2
　8
　1

4 into 9 hundreds gives 2 hundreds and we have 100 over, *i.e.,* we shall have two

Notes

54. in U.S. currency—e.g., $6.48 ÷ 2 = $3.24

Long Division *breaks a division problem down into a sequence of steps written down in detail. When the divisor is a small number,* **Short Division** *can be used, going through the sequence of steps mentally.*

56. in U.S. currency—Say that this is a new way of putting down division problems, so that we can see the Remainder after dividing into dollars, dimes, and pennies; or hundreds, tens, and units.

Arithmetic

Notes

In the division format used today, the equation would look something like this

```
         231
    4 ) 924
         8
        12
        12
         4
         4
```

hundreds in our answer. What shall we do with this 100? Analogy with subtraction will perhaps lead the children to suggest that it should be turned into tens, though we are almost certain to have the question 'Why can't you divide 100 by 4?' That would be dividing 100 units, and we must find out how many tens there are in the answer before doing the units. We then have ten tens and two others to add in, *i.e.*, 12 tens into which 4 will divide 3 tens times, we shall have 3 *tens* in the answer, and into the 4 units left 4 will divide once, so that the sum stands—

```
   4)924(231.  Answer
     8
     ___
     1       hundred
    10
    ___
    10       tens
    +2
    ___
    12       tens
    12
    ___
     4       units
     4
     ___
```

(Stephens, 1911, p. 12).

57. In order to give the children a complete idea of division, fractions are looked at briefly. First, the relationship between giving away a fraction of something and dividing it into parts then giving a part away is explored.

"The other aspect of division, *e.g.*, that suggesting fractions, is now taken. If I had 8 oranges and gave away half of them, how many would that be? How many if I gave away one-quarter? If I had 9 and gave away one-third? This last probably gets no answer at first. What did giving away one-half mean? Dividing into 2 parts and giving away 1. What then do you think giving away one *third* would mean? Dividing into 3 equal parts and giving one away? Yes, so we divide 9 into 3 equal parts and give 1 away. The third, one-half, one-quarter are written ⅓, ½, ¼, and mean 1 of 3 parts, 1 of 2 parts, 1 of 4 parts, ⅕ would mean one of 5 parts" (Stephens, 1911, p. 12).

58. Second, children find simple fractions of numbers by using a variety of manipulatives and dividing them into heaps.

"Now we give many problems, all involving the use of simple apparatus, pennies, pencils, nuts; asking the children for simple fractions, ⅕, ⅓, ¼ of numbers and letting them obtain the answer by dividing into heaps" (Stephens, 1911, p. 12).

59. When the children can articulate the correlation between simple fractions and division, mental math—little problems worked orally—is incorporated.

"Then one obtains from them the information that ⅕ of 20 equals 4 and 20 ÷ 5 = 4, so that ¼ of 20 means 20 ÷ 4, and one gives them a number of simple sums to be worked orally, and introduces them to the notation for farthings in English money sums" (Stephens, 1911, p. 13).

A farthing was a British coin equal to ¼ of a penny. It is no longer in use.

60. Fractions are addressed only briefly at this time in order to give the

children a complete idea of division. Fractions will be revisited once decimals have been learned.

"The subject of fractions is left here; it is only touched upon at all in order to give the children a complete notion of division; the subject is not taken up again until the children have mastered decimals" (Stephens, 1911, p. 13).

Weights and Measures

61. The formal study of Weights and Measures begins around nine years of age, completing elementary arithmetic.

"This part of the subject is reached at the beginning of the average child's ninth year, and is the concluding part of the course in elementary arithmetic" (Stephens, 1911, p. 13).

62. The learning of weights and measures is done with a hands-on approach. By making up parcels of differing weights using a scale and various materials, the child exercises judgment while fostering habits of accuracy, neatness, and skillfulness.

"If the child do not get the ground under his feet at this stage, he works arithmetic ever after by rule of thumb. On the same principle, let him learn 'weights and measures' by measuring and weighing; let him have scales and weights, sand or rice, paper and twine, and weigh, and do up, in *perfectly* made parcels, ounces, pounds, etc. The *parcels*, though they are not arithmetic, are educative, and afford considerable exercise of judgment as well as of neatness, deftness, and quickness" (Vol. 1, pp. 259, 260).

63. The child makes his own tables, weighing things that are clean and easy to handle like water or sand.

"The child weighs and measures for himself and makes his own tables; we let him, dressed in a pinafore, measure out pints and quarts of water, very careful not to spill anything, and weigh pounds and ounces of sand or anything clean and easily handled" (Stephens, 1911, p. 13).

64. First work with the units of measure used in your country.

"Our own weights and measures, of which they have probably heard, are taken first" (Stephens, 1911, p. 13).

65. A hands-on approach to weights and measures prepares the child for the idea of fractions.

"While engaged in measuring and weighing concrete quantities, the scholar is prepared to take in his first idea of a 'fraction,' half a pound, a quarter of a yard, etc." (Vol. 1, p. 260).

66. Not everything can be weighed or measured in a home schoolroom. Explain to the child that large weights, such as tons, are used for weighing

> *Cwt. stands for "hundred-weight."*

very heavy things like cars and trucks. These should also then be added to his table.

"There are, of course, limitations to schoolroom weighing and measuring: tons and cwt., they are told, are the big weights used when men want to weigh very heavy things like beams of iron; and these weights are added to the table already made from drams to pounds" (Stephens, 1911, p. 13).

67. The child should work with a 1-foot ruler and yardstick in the same way, drawing up his own tables.

"In like manner, let him work with foot-rule and yard measure, and draw up his tables for himself" (Vol. 1, p. 260).

68. Once tables have been drawn up, children will read through them a number of times. Oral questions are given in quick succession and then written problems are worked.

"After the tables have been made the children read through them once or twice and then have a number of rapid oral questions. How many ounces in two pounds? In 1 lb. 10 oz.? How many cwts. in 1 ton 6 cwt.? &c., &c., and then a large number of problems to be worked in their books" (Stephens, 1911, p. 13).

69. Metric tables are now introduced. The ease with which the decimal system is applied, along with the sensibility of working in tens, make for enjoyable lessons in this area.

"The metric tables are given as those used in other countries, and the children take to them as ducks to water; every British teacher of arithmetic must bemoan the fact of British weights and measures. With our adoption of a decimal system of coinage and measurement a great deal of what seems such unnecessary labour on his or her part will be saved; the rational and logical aspect of this work in tens seems to appeal to the children as well as to the teacher, and they are always delighted when metric measures are involved in their sums" (Stephens, 1911, p. 13).

70. As much as possible, hands-on problems are worked. Children may measure objects in the room as well as things outside. Measurements are done in both conventional (Imperial or U.S) and metric units, making a table of comparative weights and measures.

"The children work practical problems as much as possible at this stage, measuring the girth of trees, the furniture of the schoolroom, &c., and making thus a table of comparative weights and measures; metric expressed in British units and *vice versa*" (Stephens, 1911, p. 13).

71. Now is also the time to exercise a child's judgment with questions pertaining to weight and measurement. This promotes an eager readiness within the child that is worth nurturing.

"Let him not only measure and weigh everything about him that admits of such treatment, but let him use his judgment on questions of measure and weight. How many yards long is the tablecloth? how many feet long and broad a map, or picture? What does he suppose a book weighs that is to go by parcel post? The sort of readiness to be gained thus is valuable in the affairs of life, and, if only for that reason, should be cultivated in the child" (Vol. 1, p. 260).

72. By placing objects in comparison to other objects, a child realizes how calling something "heavy" or "light" changes. This comparison, shown through a series of questions, helps cultivate accuracy and truth in an enjoyable way.

"Care in this matter makes for higher moral, as well as intellectual development: half the dissensions in the world arise from an indiscriminate use of epithets. 'Would you say your bread (at dinner) was light or heavy?' The child would probably answer, 'Rather light.' 'Yes, we can only say that a thing is light by comparing it with others; what is bread light compared with?' 'A stone, a piece of coal, of cheese, of butter of the same size.' 'But it is heavy compared with?' 'A piece of sponge cake, a piece of sponge, of cork, of pumice,' and so on. 'What do you think it weighs?' 'An ounce,' 'an ounce and a half.' 'We'll try after dinner; you had better have another piece and save it,' and the weighing after dinner is a delightful operation. The power of judging of weight is worth cultivating. We heard the other day of a gentleman who was required at a bazaar to guess the weight of a monster cake; he poised it and said it weighed eighteen pounds fourteen ounces, and it did exactly. *Caeteris paribus*, one has a greater respect for the man who made this accurate judgment than for the vague person, who suggested that the cake might weigh ten pounds" (Vol. 2, p. 184).

73. Incidental lessons that exercise a child's judgment as to weight can take place at any time and anywhere. Without using a scale, weight is judged using the sense of touch, and children gradually realize how an object's weight depends upon its density.

"Letters, book parcels, an apple, an orange, a vegetable marrow, fifty things in the course of the day, give opportunities for this kind of object teaching; *i.e.* the practice of forcing judgments as to the relative and absolute weight of objects by the irresistance, that is their opposition to our muscular force, perceived by our sense of touch. By degrees the children are trained to observe that the relative weights of objects depend upon their relative density, and are introduced to the fact that we have a standard of weight" (Vol. 2, pp. 184, 185).

74. Judgment of size is secured in the same way. With a series of questions using everyday objects, children measure by eye and then must confirm their judgment. This exercise promotes what is called a "good eye."

"In the same way children should be taught to measure objects by the eye. How high is that candlestick? How long and broad that picture-frame? and so on—verifying their statements. What is the circumference of that bowl? of the clock-face? of that flower-bed? How tall is So-and-so, and So-and-so? How many hands high are the horses of their acquaintance? Divide a slip of wood, a sheet of paper into halves, thirds, quarters by the eye; lay a walking-stick at right angles with another; detect when a picture, curtain, etc., hangs out of the perpendicular. This sort of practice will secure for children what is called a correct, or true, eye" (Vol. 2, p. 185).

Notes

Caeteris paribus is Latin for "all things being equal."

Measure of Area

75. Children are asked how to tell how big something is altogether, not just how long or wide it is. They are thus led to discover the rule for finding area *through a series of steps.*

1. Have the child first look at a sheet of graph paper divided up into squares and count the squares. The page is so many squares big.
2. Next have the child draw a picture of a book six squares long and five squares wide. Ask, "How big is it?" "30 squares big, because there are five rows each containing six squares."
3. Do this exercise with the child drawing various objects such as a book or pencil case.
4. Explain that if the squares were 1 inch long and 1 inch wide it would be called a square inch; if it were 1 foot long and 1 foot wide it would be called a square foot. Dividing walls, floors and other things up into square feet or square inches will tell how big it is, which is called area.
5. Now draw a number of rectangles on paper divided into square inches. Find the area by counting the number of rows and number of squares. Show the progression:

   Area = 5 rows of 2 squares each.
        = 5 x 2 squares.
        = 10 squares or 10 square inches.

"How should we be able to tell how big the wall is, or the floor? We can tell how long the picture rail is, how *long* and how *wide* the door, but we must get a new way of telling how big it is altogether. Look at a page of your arithmetic book; it is divided up into squares, and you can tell how big it is by counting the squares. Draw a picture of a book 6 squares long and 5 squares wide. How big is it? 30 squares big, because there are 5 rows each containing 6 squares. Draw the top of a pencil box 2 squares wide and 10 squares long; there are 2 rows of 10 squares each; it is 20 squares big. Now suppose we have each square 1 inch long and 1 inch wide, it is then called a square inch; if we had it 1 foot long and 1 foot wide we should call it a square foot, and we measure walls and doors by dividing them up into square feet or square inches. This kind of bigness is called *area*. We draw many rectangular figures on paper divided into square inches, and find the area of each by counting the number of rows and number of squares in each, *e.g.*, a rectangle 5 inches long and 2 inches wide.

    area = 5 rows of 2 squares each.
          = 5 × 2 squares.
          = 10 squares or 10 square inches" (Stephens, 1911, p. 14).

76. After the child has worked out the rule for finding area, he should make a table of square yards, feet, and inches and measure the area of things around the house such as a map, windows, or doors. After completing work in the concrete, a number of problems are worked in his book.

"Thus the children finally arrive at the rule for finding areas, and then make themselves a table of square yards, feet, and inches. They now measure and find the area of hearthstones, windows, steps, blackboards, &c., and work numerous problems in their books" (Stephens, 1911, p. 14).

77. The same steps are repeated for metric square measure and cubic measure.

"Metric square measure is taken in the same way, *i.e.,* by measuring rectangles divided into centimetre squares, and by measuring the furniture of their schoolroom in metres and centimetres.

"*Cubic Measure* has to be taken in much the same way as square measure, dice or cubes of some sort serving for the preliminary stage, which is shorter than with square measure" (Stephens, 1911, p. 14).

78. Elementary Arithmetic spans the first four school years, and is characterized by thorough, careful work in which the children make discoveries for themselves.

"This concludes the fourth year of school life with the ordinary child, and though he has not perhaps progressed very rapidly or "done" many rules and varieties of sums, he has worked thoroughly and discovered much for himself" (Stephens, 1911, p. 14).

More Thoughts on Arithmetic

1. Arithmetic lessons are not coordinated with other studies through arbitrary connections.

"Another point, the co-ordination of studies is carefully regulated without any reference to the clash of ideas on the threshold or their combination into apperception masses; but solely with reference to the natural and inevitable co-ordination of certain subjects. Thus, in readings on the period of the Armada, we should not devote the contemporary arithmetic lessons to calculations as to the amount of food necessary to sustain the Spanish fleet, because this is an arbitrary and not an inherent connection; but we should read such history, travels, and literature as would make the Spanish Armada live in the mind" (Vol. 3, pp. 230, 231).

2. Charlotte offered the following for those considering utilizing her philosophy of education: no cramming for exams and an eagerness toward school work and exam preparation no matter what a child's previous manner of education.

"9. There is no distressing cramming for the term's examination. The pupils know their work, and find it easy to answer questions set to find out what they know, rather than what they do not know.

"10. Children of any age, however taught hitherto, take up this sort of work with avidity.

"11. Boys and girls taught in this way take up ordinary school work, preparation for examinations, etc., with intelligence, zeal, and success" (Vol. 3, p. 301).

"It rarely happens that all the children in a class are not able to answer all the

Notes

Johan Herbart (1776–1841) was a German philosopher who developed a system of education based on psychology and ethics. According to Herbartian belief, students were passive learners and the teacher was responsible for linking ideas together in a chain of apperception masses. For more of Charlotte's criticisms of education along Herbartian lines and examples of *correlating studies and* concentration schemes, *modernly referred to as Unit Studies, see Volume 2, pages 255 and 256, and Volume 6, pages 114–125. Charlotte also wrote about Herbart in detail, and the similarities and differences of a PNEU education, in Volume 3, chapter 9.*

Notes

N.B. *stands for* Nota Bene, *which is Latin for "Note Well." Such a designation was used to draw the attention of the reader to a particular point.*

A vulgar fraction is a common fraction, written with a numerator and a denominator, like ⅓ or ¼.

questions set in such subjects as history, literature, citizenship, geography, science. But here differences manifest themselves; some children do better in history, some in science, some in arithmetic, others in literature; some, again, write copious answers and a few write sparsely; but practically all know the answers to the set questions" (Vol. 6. p. 241).

3. Charlotte asked parents and educators to note that children should go on from where they had left off in their study of mathematics and that there should be no gaps.

"N.B. 1.—In grammar (English and foreign) and in mathematics there must be no gaps. Children must go on from where they left off, but they will be handicapped in the future unless they can do the work set for this Form" (PNEU Programmes 90–94, May–July 1921 through December 1922).

Junior Arithmetic

By the end of grade 6, children have obtained some knowledge of vulgar and decimal fractions, percentage, and household accounts.

"The six years' work—from six to twelve—which I suggest, should and does result in the power of the pupils—

"…(g) In Arithmetic, they should have some knowledge of vulgar and decimal fractions, percentage, household accounts, etc." (Vol. 3, p. 301).

Questions to Ask about Arithmetic

- Am I sure not to begin the formal study of arithmetic with my child before age six?
- Are lessons presented in a measured, deliberate way?
- Are lessons kept short, 20 minutes in the earlier years and no more than 30 minutes in the later years?
- Do I require concentrated attention from my child?
- Are problems given within my child's grasp?
- Do I allow my child to use manipulatives before progressing to the imagining of objects and then on to abstract number?
- Are the problems I give my child of an interesting nature?
- Am I sure my child's understanding is secured before moving on to the next lesson in arithmetic?
- Do we use money problems and work with real money in our lessons?
- Am I content to work slowly and steadily until my child has mastered the idea of place value?

Questions to Ask about the Four Rules and Tables

- Do I have my child work out addition and subtraction tables with concrete objects?
- Is subtraction presented as the complement to addition?

- Is multiplication introduced as repeated addition through simple problems?
- Has my child constructed a multiplication table in order to see the reason behind it?
- Do I have my child construct the multiplication table in written form as another tool to understanding its rationale?
- When my child is memorizing the multiplication table am I sure to have it learned in a variety of ways, not only in consecutive order?
- Is my child being exercised on the tables learned with interesting money problems before moving onto abstract numbers?
- Are two different meanings of division conveyed, the idea of continuous subtraction and the idea of fractional parts?
- Am I sure to bring manipulatives back out when each new rule is introduced?

Questions to Ask about Writing Problems

- Are our lessons mainly oral and writing of sums used in moderation?
- When my child does write out problems, am I sure she is keeping proper place value alignment?
- As my child advances in her study of arithmetic, am I requiring careful arrangement and neatness of written work?

Questions to Ask about Weight and Measurement

- Are we using a hands-on approach to learning weights and measures?
- Do I have my child make her own tables of weights and measures?
- Do I then exercise my child in the tables of weights and measurements through oral questions and then written problems?
- Has my child been introduced to metric tables, measuring in both conventional and metric and then making a table of comparative weights and measures?
- Do I exercise my child's judgment with questions pertaining to weight and measurement to promote readiness and a good eye?

Questions to Ask about Arithmetic in the Upper Grades

- Are lessons kept to 30 minutes?
- As my child continues her study of arithmetic, is she still receiving oral practice?
- Are long and boring calculations excluded from our lessons?
- Are problems of an interesting nature, aimed at reality?
- Is my child being taught, or is more emphasis placed on "getting through" a textbook?

Arithmetic Scope and Sequence

...dline which topics of Arithmetic were taught in which grades to Charlotte's students.
...d from PNEU programmes used up until 1923 and available at time of publication.)

	1	2	3
...te U.S. Grade	1	2	3
...ate U.S. Age	6–7	7–8	8–9
Analysis of Numbers *			
One through Nine.	x		
Meanings of Symbols.	x		
Notation	x		
The Number 10	x		
Units, Ten Bundles	x		
Eleven through Twenty	x		
Idea of Place Value	x		
Introduction of Money.	x		
Reduction of Money.	x		
Simple Money Sums	x		
Twenty through Thirty	x		
30-100 (taken in groups of ten)	x		
Understand numeration and notation up to 1000.		x	
Understand numeration and notation up to 10,000.			x
The Four Rules and Tables			
Addition			
Review previous years' work.		x	x
Understand the idea of addition.		x	
Money sums in addition.		x	x
Sums on pure number.		x	x
Longer sums with three or four sets of figures.		x	
Add numbers within 1000.		x	
Add numbers within 10,000.			x
Harder compound addition			x
Subtraction			
Review previous years' work.		x	x
Understand the idea of subtraction.		x	
Money sums.		x	x
Pure number subtraction sums.		x	x
Subtract numbers within 1000.		x	
Subtract numbers within 10,000.			x
Harder compound subtraction			x
Multiplication			
Review previous years' work.		x	x
Present as extension to addition by using repeated addition to solve problems.		x	
Simple Multiplication to show the idea of "times."		x	
Introduce the symbol "x"		x	
Construction of multiplication tables by student.		x	x
Master multiplication table up to 6x12.		x	
Master multiplication table up to 12x12.			x
Multiplication problems involving money.		x	x
Pure number multiplication with problems involving real things.		x	x
Multiplication by 10's, 100's, 1000's.		x	
Division			
Review previous years' work.		x	x
The idea of division as continuous subtraction through sharing and grouping exercises worked with manipulatives.		x	
Introduce the symbol "÷"		x	
Simple money sums involving division.		x	
Short division.		x	
Long division introduced.			x
Simple fractions introduced.			x

* i.e., investigation of each number by working out addition and subtraction sums involving its use. Initially done with the aid of manipulatives then proceeding to oral work with the writing of sums used very sparingly.

Grades 4–6

	4	5	6
Approximate U.S. Grade	4	5	6
Approximate U.S. Age	9–10	10–11	11–12
Arithmetic			
Read *Number Stories of Long Ago* by D.E. Smith in free time.	x		
Addition			
Count by twos, from 1 to 100.	x		
Count by threes, fours, etc., up to twelves, from 1-100.	x		
Oral arithmetic, adding rows of five numbers up to 100.	x		
Written arithmetic, adding columns of numbers up to ten thousands.	x		
Subtraction			
Count backwards from 20, subtracting 2 each time.	x		
Count backward from 30, subtracting threes; and so on up to 100, subtracting tens.	x		
Subtraction of rows of numbers no greater than 55.	x		
Subtraction of columns of numbers no greater than ten thousands place.	x		
Sums using brackets.	x		
Reduction of money.	x		
Harder Compound Addition using Money.	x		
Harder Compound Subtraction using Money.	x		
Multiplication			
Simple Multiplication.	x		
Areas.	x		
Short Compound Multiplication using Money.	x		
Long Multiplication.	x		
Multiplication by a Product.	x		
Rules to help get Multiplication Sums Right.	x		
Division			
Short Division.	x		
Short Division of Money.	x		
Division of one quantity by another.	x		
Averages.	x		
Long Division.	x		
Long Division of Money.	x		
Rules to help get Division Sums Right.	x		
Weights and Measures			
Measures of Length.	x		
Metric Measures of Length.	x		
Measures of Area or Square Measure.	x		
Metric Measures of Area.	x		
Measures of Volume	x		
Approximate U.S. Grade	4	5	6
Approximate U.S. Age	9–10	10–11	11–12
(Arithmetic continued)			
Decimals			
Decimals and their Meaning.	x		
Multiplication of Decimals.		x	
Division of Decimals.		x	
Dollars and cents.		x	
Approximations.		x	
Decimals of Money.		x	
Measurement by Decimals.		x	
Factors			
Measures of Numbers.		x	
Greatest Common Measure		x	
Numbers divisible by 2.		x	
Numbers divisible by 3.		x	
Numbers divisible by 4.		x	
Numbers divisible by 5.		x	
Numbers divisible by 8.		x	
Numbers divisible by 9.		x	
Numbers divisible by 11.		x	
Numbers divisible by 12.		x	
Prime Numbers.		x	
Greatest Common Measure or Highest Common Factor.		x	
Multiples of a Number.		x	
Least Common Multiple.		x	
Decimals of Money.		x	
Fractions			
Meaning.		x	
Improper Fractions.		x	
Turning Decimals into Common or Vulgar Fractions.		x	
Turnig Common or Vulgar Fractions into Decimals.		x	
Cancelling.		x	
Multiplication of Fractions.			x
Division of Fractions.			x
Review Decimals.			x
Review G.C.M., L.C.M.			x
Simple Proportion.			x
Percentages.			x
Simple Interest.			x
Review Fractions.			x

Arithmetic

Grades 7–12

Approximate U.S. Grade	7	8
Approximate Age	12–13	13–14
Arithmetic		
Read *Number Stories of Long Ago* by D.E. Smith in free time.	x	x
Compound Division of Money	x	
Division of Money by Money	x	
Weights and Measures		
Reductions of Weights and Measures	x	
Addition of Weights and Measures	x	
Subtraction of Weights and Measures	x	
Multiplication of Weights and Measures	x	
Division of Weights and Measures	x	
Factors and Prime Numbers		
Greatest Common Factor or Greatest Common Measure	x	
Least Common Multiple	x	
Review GCF and LCM		x
Fractions		
Common or Vulgar Fractions	x	
Reduction to Lowest Terms	x	
Comparison of Fractions	x	
Improper Fractions and Mixed Numbers	x	
Addition of Fractions	x	
Subtraction of Fractions	x	
Multiplication by a Whole Number	x	
Division by a Whole Number	x	
Multiplication by a Fraction	x	
Simplification: the use of brackets	x	
Concrete Quantities with Fractions	x	
Complex Fractions	x	
Problems involving Fractions	x	
Decimals		
Notation		x
Short Methods in Multiplication		x
Short Methods in Division		x
Addition of Decimals		x
Subtraction of Decimals		x
Multiplication of Decimals		x
Division of Decimals		x
Reduction of Common (Vulgar) Fractions to Decimals		x
Complex Fractions involving Decimals		x
Recurring Decimals		x
Addition and Subtraction of Recurring Decimals		x
Multiplication and Division of Recurring Decimals		x
Simple and Compound Interest		x
Working with Invoices		x
Simple Proportions		x
Compound Proportion		x
Proportionate Division		x

Approximate U.S. Grade	9	10	11	12
Approximate Age	14–15	15–16	16–17	17–18
Arithmetic				
Simple Proportion	x	x	x	x
Compound Proportion	x	x	x	x
Proportionate Division	x	x	x	x
Bankruptcies	x	x	x	x
Review Previous Work	x	x	x	x
Bankruptcies - Dividends on a Debt	x	x	x	x
Rates and Taxes	x	x	x	x
Percentages	x	x	x	x
Review Previous Work	x	x	x	x
Percentages	x	x	x	x
Commission, Brokerage, Insurance, Cash Discount	x	x	x	x
Profit and Loss	x	x	x	x
Simple Interest	x	x	x	x
Compound Interest	x	x	x	x
Review decimalization of money values	x	x	x	x
Review G.C.M. and L.C.M.	x	x	x	x
Review vulgar fractions	x	x	x	x
Review decimal fractions.	x	x	x	x
Averages and their practical application.	x	x	x	x

Note: Review exercises and more difficult exercises to be taken with each consecutive year.

Chapter 3
Manipulatives

"What does your family use for math manipulatives?" asked Heather. "I was looking at an online store and they had 16 pages of different manipulatives, and they're all so expensive."

"Don't I know it," answered Cindy. "We paid so much for our math manipulatives that I was determined to get good use out of them. It didn't take long before my son was completely bored by them. He didn't even want to take them out of the cupboard and started complaining each time he had to 'build' a problem. That's when I took a closer look at what Charlotte Mason had to say. It turns out that all we really need can be found in our own homes—beans, buttons, craft sticks, or beads to name a few."

"Then how exactly are they used, and what keeps your son from becoming bored with those as well?"

"Using a variety of objects is one key, and being sure to put manipulatives away as soon as they are no longer needed is another. Here's an example of a simple lesson in exploring the number 7. First I would have my child arrange an addition table using pennies, placing 1 penny next to 6 pennies, 2 pennies next to 5 pennies, and so on. I then pose a number of questions using pennies, such as '7 pennies + 2 pennies = how many pennies?' When he is able to answer with confidence, I progress to questions using different imaginary objects but allow him to use the pennies if needed to obtain the answer. Using a concrete object like pennies not only proves the math facts, but shows him these facts are general and not tied to the specific manipulative we're using that day. For example, I might ask:

'7 pencils plus 1 pencil equals how many pencils?'
'8 apples minus 1 apple leaves how many apples?'

and continue giving similar problems until the answers come readily. Next he is exercised in simple sums using just the numbers, such as '7 + 4 ='; and when I observe that he can answer effortlessly, without even glancing at his pennies, we put them away. From this point, he won't work with manipulatives until the next concept is introduced."

Manipulatives and the Use of Concrete Objects in Charlotte's Classrooms

Though *math manipulative* was not a term utilized in Charlotte's time, the use of concrete objects as aids in conveying ideas is significant in Mason's philosophy of education. She believed a contrived environment and specially designed apparatus were detrimental to children and instead made use of commonplace objects and simple counters. Arithmetic tables were not memorized until they were worked in the concrete with the facts first being proved.

Manipulatives

Notes

Concrete Objects or Manipulatives Mentioned in Charlotte's Writings

Bag of beans
Counters
Buttons
Fingers
Nuts
Coins in various denominations
Scales and weights
Sand
Rice
Paper and twine
Ruler
Yard measure or yard stick
Balls
Dominoes
Matchsticks
Beads
String

Charlotte's Thoughts on Using Concrete Objects

1. Concrete objects were used in all beginning arithmetic lessons, progressing to mental operations and then the working of sums.

"A bag of beans, counters, or buttons should be used in all the early arithmetic lessons, and the child should be able to work with these freely, and even to add, subtract, multiply, and divide mentally, without the aid of buttons or beans, before he is set to 'do sums' on his slate" (Vol. 1, p. 256).

2. Concrete objects demonstrate to the child both the validity of math facts and the reason for the processes used, laying the groundwork in the early stages of arithmetic for beginning mathematics. The ability to do sums or use the appropriate rules is not enough to provide a strong foundation for mathematics.

"The next point is to demonstrate everything demonstrable. The child may learn the multiplication-table and do a subtraction sum without any insight into the *rationale* of either. He may even become a good arithmetician, applying rules aptly, without seeing the reason of them; but arithmetic becomes an elementary mathematical training only in so far as the reason why of every process is clear to the child. 2+2=4, is a self-evident fact, admitting of little demonstration; but 4x7=28 may be proved" (Vol. 1, pp. 255, 256).

3. The child realizes the idea of multiplication as an extension of addition by using concrete objects to work out a multiplication fact.

"He has a bag of beans; places four rows with seven beans in a row; adds the rows, thus: 7 and 7 are 14, and 7 are 21, and 7 are 28; how many sevens in 28? 4. Therefore it is right to say 4x7=28; and the child sees that multiplication is only a short way of doing addition" (Vol. 1, p. 256).

4. Children simultaneously work out addition and subtraction tables by use of the concrete, giving the idea that subtraction is the counterpart to addition.

"He may arrange an addition table with his beans, thus—

```
0 0   0      =  3 beans
0 0   0 0    =  4   "
0 0   0 0 0  =  5   "
```

and be exercised upon it until he can tell, first without counting, and then without looking at the beans, that 2+7=9, etc.

"Thus with 3, 4, 5,—each of the digits: as he learns each line of his addition table he is exercised upon imaginary objects, '4 apples and 9 apples,' '4 nuts and 6 nuts,' etc.; and lastly, with abstract numbers—6+5, 6+8.

"A subtraction table is worked out simultaneously with the addition table. As he works out each line of additions, he goes over the same ground, only taking away one bean, or two beans, instead of adding, until he is able to answer quite readily, 2 from 7? 2 from 5? . . . It will be found that it requires a much greater mental effort on the child's part to grasp the idea of subtraction than that of addition, and the teacher must be content to go slowly—one finger from four fingers, one nut from three nuts, and so forth, until he knows what he is about" (Vol. 1, pp. 256, 257).

5. Multiplication and division tables are introduced using concrete objects.

"When the child can add and subtract numbers pretty freely up to twenty, the multiplication and division tables may be worked out with beans, as far as 6x12; that is, 'twice six are 12' will be ascertained by means of two rows of beans, six beans in a row.

"When the child can say readily, without even a glance at his beans, 2x8=16, 2x7=14, etc., he will take 4, 6, 8, 10, 12 beans, and divide them into groups of two: then, how many twos in 10, in 12, in 20? And so on, with each line of the multiplication table that he works out" (Vol. 1, p. 257).

6. Children are encouraged to discard the concrete by working with imaginary objects before advancing to abstract numbers.

"Now he is ready for more ambitious problems: thus, 'A boy had twice ten apples; how many heaps of 4 could he make?' He will be able to work with promiscuous numbers, as 7+5-3. If he must use beans to get his answer, let him; but encourage him to work with *imaginary* beans, as a step towards working with abstract numbers. Carefully graduated teaching and *daily* mental effort on the child's part at this early stage may be the means of developing real mathematical power, and will certainly promote the habits of concentration and effort of mind" (Vol. 1, p. 257).

7. Working with coins is the first step in understanding our system of notation in arithmetic. The idea of changing units to tens comes to the child easily after having changed pennies into dimes, or pence into shillings in Charlotte's time.

"When the child is able to work pretty freely with small numbers, a serious difficulty must be faced, upon his thorough mastery of which will depend his

Notes

At the time of Charlotte's writing there were 12 pence, or pennies, in a shilling and 240 pence, or 20 shillings, in a pound. The United Kingdom decimalized their currency system in 1971.

7. in U.S. currency— Let him have a heap of pennies, say fifty-seven: point out the inconvenience of carrying such weighty money to stores. Lighter money is used—dimes. How many pennies is a dime worth? How many dimes, then, might he have for his fifty-seven pennies? He divides them into heaps of ten, and finds that he has five such heaps. Fifty-seven cents are (or are worth) five dimes and seven pennies. I buy five gumballs at 5¢ apiece; they cost twenty-five cents; show the child how to put down: the pennies, which are worth least, to the right; the dimes, which are worth more, to the left.
When the child is working freely with dimes and pennies, and understands that a 2 in the right-hand column of figures is pennies, and a 2 in the left-hand column, dimes, introduce the idea of tens and units, being content to work slowly and steadily.

apprehension of arithmetic as a science; in other words, will depend the educational value of all the sums he may henceforth do. He must be made to understand our system of notation. Here, as before, it is best to begin with the concrete: let the child get the idea of ten *units* in one *ten* after he has mastered the more easily demonstrable idea of twelve pence in one shilling.

"Let him have a heap of pennies, say fifty: point out the inconvenience of carrying such weighty money to shops. Lighter money is used—shillings. How many pennies is a shilling worth? How many shillings, then, might he have for his fifty pennies? He divides them into heaps of twelve, and finds that he has four such heaps, and two pennies over; that is to say, fifty pence are (or are worth) four shillings and twopence. I buy ten pounds of biscuits at fivepence a pound; they cost fifty pence, but the shopman gives me a bill for 4*s*. 2*d*.; show the child how to put down: the pennies, which are worth least, to the right; the shillings, which are worth more, to the left.

"When the child is able to work freely with shillings and pence, and to understand that 2 in the right-hand column of figures is pence, 2 in the left-hand column, shillings, introduce him to the notion of tens and units, being content to work very gradually" (Vol. 1, pp. 257, 258).

8. Weighing and measuring concrete quantities trains the child in exercising judgment and the habits of precision and neatness, and prepares him for the idea of fractions.

"On the same principle, let him learn 'weights and measures' by measuring and weighing; let him have scales and weights, sand or rice, paper and twine, and weigh, and do up, in *perfectly* made parcels, ounces, pounds, etc. The *parcels*, though they are not arithmetic, are educative, and afford considerable exercise of judgment as well as of neatness, deftness, and quickness. In like manner, let him work with foot-rule and yard measure, and draw up his tables for himself. Let him not only measure and weigh everything about him that admits of such treatment, but let him use his judgment on questions of measure and weight. How many yards long is the tablecloth? how many feet long and broad a map, or picture? What does he suppose a book weighs that is to go by parcel post? The sort of readiness to be gained thus is valuable in the affairs of life, and, if only for that reason, should be cultivated in the child. While engaged in measuring and weighing concrete quantities, the scholar is prepared to take in his first idea of a 'fraction,' half a pound, a quarter of a yard, etc." (Vol. 1, pp. 259, 260).

9. Though children get the basic truth of number by means of their senses, there is a natural progression from concrete to abstract thinking. After handling concrete objects or manipulatives for a time, a child is then able to envision a number of objects until he begins to think in numbers and not objects.

Complicated or elaborate apparatus are a hindrance as they involve too much teaching and direct instruction. Excessive emphasis is placed on the object rather than the number it is meant to represent.

Commonplace objects or illustrations on a blackboard can help a child get an idea of a large number, but seeing a symbol of a large number and working with the symbol are completely different things.

"I should like to refer the reader to the *A B C Arithmetic* by Messrs Sonnenschein & Nesbit. The authors found their method upon the following passage from Mill's *Logic*:—'The fundamental truths of the science of Number all rest on the evidence of sense; they are proved by showing to our eyes and our fingers that any given number of objects, ten balls for example, may by separation and re-arrangement exhibit to our senses all the different sets of numbers the sum of which is equal to ten. All the improved methods of teaching arithmetic to children proceed on a knowledge of this fact. All who wish to carry the child's *mind* along with them in learning arithmetic, all who wish to teach numbers and not mere ciphers, now teach it through the evidence of the senses in the manner we have described.'

"Here we may, I think, trace the solitary source of weakness in a surpassingly excellent manual. It is quite true that the fundamental truths of the science of number all rest on the evidence of sense; but, having used eyes and fingers upon ten balls or twenty balls, upon ten nuts, or leaves, or sheep, or what not, the child has formed the association of a given number with objects, and is able to conceive of the association of various other numbers with objects. In fact, he begins to *think* in numbers and not in objects, that is, he begins mathematics. Therefore I incline to think that an elaborate system of staves, cubes, etc., instead of tens, hundreds, thousands, errs by embarrassing the child's mind with too much teaching, and by making the illustration occupy a more prominent place than the thing illustrated.

"Dominoes, beans, graphic figures drawn on the blackboard, and the like, are, on the other hand, aids to the child when it is necessary for him to conceive of a great number with the material of a small one; but to see a symbol of the great numbers and to work with such a symbol are quite different matters" (Vol. 1, pp. 261, 262).

Notes

The book referred to is A System of Logic: Ratiocinative and Inductive *by British utilitarian philosopher and naturalist, John Stuart Mill. Published in 1843, the book is commonly known as Mill's* Logic. *Charlotte Mason found utilitarian education "profoundly immoral" (Vol. 3, pp. 240, 241).*

10. Overexposure to geometrical forms and figures in an artificial way, either through continuous display or play, results in boredom and an aversion to the objects rather than an affinity toward mathematics.

"In the 'forties' and 'fifties' it was currently held that the continual sight of the outward and visible signs (geometrical forms and figures) should beget the inward and spiritual grace of mathematical genius, or, at any rate, of an inclination to mathematics. But the educationalists of those days forgot, when they gave children boxes of 'form' and stuck up cubes, hexagons, pentagons, and what not, in every available schoolroom space, the immense capacity for being bored which is common to us all, and is far more strongly developed in children than in grown-up people. The objects which bore us, or the persons who bore us, appear to wear a bald place in the mind, and thought turns from them with sick aversion. Dickens showed us the pathos of it in the schoolroom of the little Gradgrinds, which was bountifully supplied with objects of uncompromising outline. Ruskin, more genially, exposes the fallacy. No doubt geometric forms abound,—the skeletons of which living beauty, in contour and gesture, in hill and plant, is the covering; and the skeleton is beautiful and wonderful to the mind which has already entered within the portals of geometry. But children should not be presented with the skeleton, but with the living forms which clothe it" (Vol. 1, p. 263).

The little Gradgrinds were the children of Thomas Gradgrind in Charles Dickens' 1854 serial novel, Hard Times. *In the novel, a measure of Dickens' satire was aimed at radical utilitarians in the character of Thomas Gradgrind, a rigid headmaster who believed children were empty vessels to be filled with facts. Gradgrind's own children received an education based in fact only. Nothing was allowed to ignite their imagination and their schoolroom was appropriately outfitted with this aim in mind.*

11. Direct preparation for mathematics, that is, exposing children to geometrical forms at an early age in the hopes of developing mathematical brilliance, is undesirable. Form is the outcome of the idea and not vice versa.

Notes

Charlotte sometimes referred to the child's mind as "spiritual" to convey her belief that it was not a mere container to fill, but an invisible living organism that can "digest" ideas as a physical body digests its food. One of her foundational 20 principles is "10. On the contrary, a child's mind is no mere sac to hold ideas; but is rather, if the figure may be allowed, a spiritual *organism, with an appetite for all knowledge. This is its proper diet, with which it is prepared to deal, and which it can digest and assimilate as the body does foodstuffs" (Vol. 1, Preface).*

"Besides, is it not an inverse method to familiarise the child's eye with patterns made by his compasses, or stitched upon his card, in the hope that the form will beget the idea? For the novice, it is probably the rule that the idea must beget the form, and any suggestion of an idea from a form comes only to the initiated. I do not think that any direct preparation for mathematics is desirable. The child, who has been allowed to think and not compelled to cram, hails the new study with delight when the due time for it arrives. The reason why mathematics are a great study is because there exists in the normal mind an affinity and capacity for this study; and too great an elaboration, whether of teaching or of preparation, has, I think, a tendency to take the edge off this manner of intellectual interest" (Vol. 1, pp. 263, 264).

12. An over-reliance upon apparatus deadens the mind and is among the causes of failure in attempting an intellectual education.

"To sum up, I believe that our efforts at intellectual education commonly fail from six causes:—

". . . (e) In elementary schools, the dependence upon apparatus and illustrative appliances which have a paralysing effect on the mind" (Vol. 3, pp. 242, 243).

13. Material objects, play, and environment are fine but are not the way to the mind. The child, as a person, must be educated with ideas.

"An authoritative saying which we are apt to associate with the religious life only is equally applicable to education. That which is born of the flesh, is flesh, we are told; but we have forgotten this great principle in our efforts at schooling children. We give them a 'play way' and play is altogether necessary and desirable but is not the avenue which leads to mind. We give them a fitting environment, which is again altogether desirable and, again, is not the way to mind. We teach them beautiful motion and we do well, for the body too must have its education; but we are not safe if we take these by-paths as approaches to mind. It is still true that that which is born of the spirit, is spirit. The way to mind is a quite direct way. Mind must come into contact with mind through the medium of ideas. 'What is mind?' says the old conundrum, and the answer still is 'No matter.' It is necessary for us who teach to realize that things material have little effect upon mind, because there are still among us schools in which the work is altogether material and technical, whether the teaching is given by means of bars of wood or more scientific apparatus" (Vol. 6, pp. 38, 39).

Questions to Ask about Concrete Objects and Manipulatives

- Am I allowing my child enough time to work with manipulatives before advancing to imaginary objects?
- Once the child can mentally picture the number or has grasped the abstract, am I sure to put the manipulative away until the introduction of a new concept?
- Has my child proven math facts by use of the concrete before being asked to commit them to memory?
- Is my child becoming bored with manipulatives?

- Are the manipulatives simple and varied so my child is able to separate the general from the specific?
- Is the manipulative a tool to the presentation or investigation of an idea, or has it become the master by requiring too much teaching or by replacing in importance the idea it is to represent?

Notes

Chapter 4
Mental Arithmetic and Oral Work

Amy glanced up at the clock—with just over five minutes remaining for the math lesson, she asked her daughter Mariah to put away the beads she had been using. The space now cleared, Amy began: "I have four cents in one pocket and two cents in the other. How many have I altogether?"

"You have six cents," Mariah replied, "because four cents plus two cents equals six cents."

Amy had helped her daughter become accustomed to giving fully-worded answers by simply asking, "Why?" if she answered with only the sum. She was also sure to pose interesting questions with relevance to everyday life and continued:

"Your little brother is three years old. How old will he be in four years?"

"How old will he be in six years?"

"Lydia wants to give her aunt, her mother, and her grandmother each a flower. She has already picked one flower, how many more shall she pick?"

"At the farmers' market, a head of broccoli costs $2. I need to purchase two heads. How much should I give the vendor?"

". . . And if I gave him $5, how much would I receive back in change?"

Mariah was enjoying the activity and promptly answered each question accurately, so Amy moved on to abstract numbers:

"5 and 3 are how many?"

"7 and 1 are how many?"

With the lesson over, Amy instructed her daughter to fetch her sewing project.

"Mom, now I have a question for you," Mariah stated, poising her needle and thread in mid-air. "At the farmers' market, chocolate pastries cost just $1. If you bought one for each member of the family, how much money should you give the baker?

"Five dollars" answered Amy.

Completing her stitch, Mariah giggled, "And how many times happier would we be than if you had spent the money on broccoli?"

Mental Arithmetic and Oral Work in Charlotte's Classrooms

Mental arithmetic and oral work were fundamental in Charlotte Mason's classrooms. Mental arithmetic is the all-important step between demonstration with the concrete and realization of the abstract. Its use reinforces math facts and vocabulary while training children in both mental and moral habits such as accuracy and steadfast thinking.

In Charlotte's classrooms oral exercises were used alongside manipulatives, and the teacher was content to go slowly with children, allowing them to prove facts

Notes

Information compiled from PNEU Programmes and Time-tables, http://www.amblesideonline.org/library.shtml#pneuprogrammes and Charlotte Mason Digital Collection, http://www.redeemer.ca/charlotte-mason.

through the use of the concrete before moving on to oral work using imaginary objects. The deliberateness of these early lessons secured prompt and accurate execution in the future, and once tables were learned, children were exercised upon them with a series of rapid oral questions before moving on to book work. Mental arithmetic or rapid oral work was also a scheduled activity, beginning with engaging word problems then progressing to oral work with pure number.

In the Programmes for Charlotte's Parents' Union School we find listed "Rapid mental work" in the first grade and "Tables up to twelve times twelve (five minutes exercise in every lesson)" for grades 2 and 3. "Tables to be worked out in money thus: 9 × 7 = 63. 63 pence = 5*q*. 3*d*." "Mental Arithmetic and Numeration for five minutes on alternate days" as well as "Rapid oral work" is given in grades 4–6, and grades 7 and 8 continued Mental Arithmetic three times a week for ten minutes at a time. "Exercises in Mental Arithmetic" found in *Arithmetic for Children* by A. E. A. Mair was specifically mentioned in Charlotte's programmes for use with the advanced years of Form II. Exercises could be found in textbooks, and teachers were also encouraged to use their own inventiveness in coming up with mental exercises, while children likely participated by adding to the line of questioning.

1. Mental arithmetic is instrumental in training both mental and moral habits.

"Give him short sums, in words rather than in figures, and excite in him the enthusiasm which produces concentrated attention and rapid work. Let his arithmetic lesson be to the child a daily exercise in clear thinking and rapid, careful execution, and his mental growth will be as obvious as the sprouting of seedlings in the spring" (Vol. 1, p. 261).

Quotes cited Pridham *refer to Pridham, Amy, "Mental Arithmetic,"* The Parents' Review, *Volume 8 (1897): pp. 112–118, http://www.amblesideonline.org/PR/PR08p112MentalArithmetic.shtml.*

"The teaching of mental arithmetic can be used to train our children in mental habits which shall lead to steadfast, accurate thinking; how it may serve as a discipline for the powers of attention, concentration and abstraction, and how it may help to train them to a love of independent and honest work.

"Mental Arithmetic can be made to produce—Fixed attention, Independent work, Promptness, Exactness. It is very early learnt that 'nearly right' won't do in this subject, and you will agree that to train our children in accuracy is of importance for every department of life" (Pridham, 1897, p. 118).

" 'How much left if you take 3 from 5?' 'How much to be added to 4 to make 7?,' and so on, quick question and quick answer, all easy and simple, so that the children may feel at home with the numbers, and feel that they have a real grasp of undoubtedly a function of some minds only, yet it, like an ear for music, can, to a certain extent, be cultivated, to a very limited extent it may be, but even that is worth striving after with our pupils" (Stephens, 1911, p. 2).

Habits Mental Arithmetic Can Help Cultivate

Concentration
Effort of mind

Attention
> Fixed Attention
> Concentrated Attention

Rapid work
Clear thinking
Careful execution
Steadfast thinking
Accurate thinking
Abstraction
Independent work
Honest work
Promptness
Exactness
Accuracy

2. In the child's early years, Charlotte did not urge any preparation for mathematics other than that which would come in a normal way through his or her surroundings. Mental Arithmetic was no exception to this rule.

"To take some very every-day examples from home life, Mental Arithmetic is beginning when you play at 'This little pig went to market.' When you divide an orange for distribution among the little ones. When you say one shoe is missing of Tommy's best pair. When the children help lay the nursery tea and count the things wanted . . . .When he can show you one brick, or three, or two as you ask for them, try whether he can imagine other things numbered with the help of bricks, finally try if he can do without bricks altogether by such questions as—If there were three little children in one room, two of them boys, how many girls? One. If you had one rose and wanted three how many more must you pick? Two" (Pridham, 1897, pp.113, 114).

3. When the regular systematic teaching of arithmetic has begun, mental arithmetic and oral work are fundamental in learning what it is to add, subtract, multiply, and divide. A natural step in moving from the concrete to the abstract, mental and oral work also precedes written work.

"A bag of beans, counters, or buttons should be used in all the early arithmetic lessons, and the child should be able to work with these freely, and even to add, subtract, multiply, and divide mentally, without the aid of buttons or beans, before he is set to 'do sums' on his slate" (Vol. 1, p. 256).

"The children do no homework at all, and their arithmetic is therefore very largely oral work" (Stephens, 1911, p. 6).

4. The step between working with concrete objects to abstract thinking is the ability to envision a number of objects.

"It is quite true that the fundamental truths of the science of number all rest on the evidence of sense; but, having used eyes and fingers upon ten balls or twenty balls, upon ten nuts, or leaves, or sheep, or what not, the child has formed the association of a given number with objects, and is able to conceive of the association

Notes

of various other numbers with objects. In fact, he begins to *think* in numbers and not in objects, that is, he begins mathematics" (Vol. 1, p. 262).

5. Each line of the addition table is learned through the use of concrete objects progressing to imaginary objects, or—in today's language—manipulatives are replaced with mental manipulatives before the child advances to working with abstract numbers.

"He may arrange an addition table with his beans, thus—

0 0   0   = 3 beans

0 0   0 0   = 4 "

0 0   0 0 0 = 5 "

and be exercised upon it until he can tell, first without counting, and then without looking at the beans, that 2+7=9, etc.

"Thus with 3, 4, 5,—each of the digits: as he learns each line of his addition table, he is exercised upon imaginary objects, '4 apples and 9 apples,' '4 nuts and 6 nuts,' etc.; and lastly, with abstract numbers—6+5, 6+8." (Vol. 1, p. 256).

"Each number is begun from a concrete set of things, beads, &c., and several questions are asked and answered with the help of the beads. Then these are put away, and for the next lesson work is done on the number without the aid of the concrete" (Stephens, 1911, p. 2).

"He will be able to work with promiscuous numbers, as 7+5-3. If he must use beans to get his answer, let him; but encourage him to work with *imaginary* beans, as a step towards working with abstract numbers" (Vol. 1, p. 257).

6. As a rule, beginning work is done orally. Though children are not yet working out written sums, they may write the answer to a sum down in their book that they will have first worked out orally.

"The sums are of course always worked orally first, and then written down, e.g., if your little sister is two years old now, how old will she be in two more years? When the answer 4 has been obtained the children write in their books 2+2=4; then they read it; two years added to two years make four years. This writing of sums, however, is very sparingly used, and all the work is oral" (Stephens, 1911, p. 2).

"My experience of children has led me to believe that if they have been thoroughly drilled in the low numbers, that is to say can add, subtract, divide and multiply and give the simpler fractional parts of any numbers up to 9, in all possible ways, without any calculations in written figures, all future work has had a good road paved for it. My reason for stopping at 9 is, that though the children do not work with written figures they certainly should be taught the symbol for the number they use, and the answer to Mental Arithmetic questions should often be written instead of given orally; in class teaching this is, of course, an immense save of time" (Pridham, 1897, p. 115).

7. When children seem perceptive and eager, mental arithmetic can progress from mental manipulatives—*that is, the imagination of objects—to pure number, helping to cultivate their comfort with numbers and the power of abstraction.*

"During this stage too we give occasional examples dealing with pure number; there are mornings when the little ones are bright and eager, and more than ever anxious to do innumerable sums; this is an opportunity to be seized by the teacher; let us leave the boxes of beads and counters alone, let us even leave out sheep and motor cars, and have nothing but numbers. 'How much left if you take 3 from 5?' 'How much to be added to 4 to make 7?,' and so on, quick question and quick answer, all easy and simple, so that the children may feel at home with the numbers, and feel that they have a real grasp of undoubtedly a function of some minds only, yet it, like an ear for music, can, to a certain extent, be cultivated, to a very limited extent it may be, but even that is worth striving after with our pupils" (Stephens, 1911, p. 2).

8. While children advance in their understanding, the questions should always remain within their comprehension.

"Engage the child upon little problems within his comprehension from the first, rather than upon set sums" (Vol. 1, p. 254).

"The examples given, though of an interesting nature, are often much too hard for the children. Their acquaintance with the science of number is still in its first stages; their work is largely oral, and the examples we find it best to give them have therefore to necessitate for their solution one arithmetical operation performed once only; addition, subtraction, or whatever it may be, e.g., 'John had 1*s.* more than Mary, he gave her 1*d.* How much had he then more than Mary?' is too difficult a question for a pupil who is just unraveling the mysteries of the number 12" (Stephens, 1911, p. 6).

"Subtraction is introduced as addition was, by little money sums practically presented at first, e.g., (a) if I have 6*d.* in my purse and give a porter 2*d.* for carrying a parcel, how much have I left; or (b) If I have six nuts and I want 9, how many more must I get?" (Stephens, 1911, p. 8).

"It is a good plan in preparing these little exercises to keep the four rules well in mind, e.g., Division: A boy had eight chestnuts and four friends, he shared them equally, how many each? Multiplication: There were three little girls, they each sang two songs, how many songs altogether? Etc." (Pridham, 1897, p. 115).

"Now he is ready for more ambitious problems: thus, 'A boy had twice ten apples; how many heaps of 4 could he make?' " (Vol. 1, p. 257).

"Now for a slightly more advanced stage. Children will work readily with mental pictures in this way:
　Walking down a street there is—　A policeman,
　　　　　　　　　　　　　　　　A dog, and
　　　　　　　　　　　　　　　　A butcher's boy.

Notes

This example involves the operation of changing shillings to pence before performing subtraction and comes from Irene Stephens' suggestions on the altering of Sonnenschein & Nesbitt's ABC of Arithmetic *if it is to be used for the early stages of teaching elementary arithmetic.*

Mental Arithmetic

Notes

How many creatures?
How many legs?
Why?" (Pridham, 1897, p. 114).

9. Have children form answers in complete sentences when doing this type of mental work.

"When the answer 4 has been obtained [orally] the children write in their books 2+2=4; then they read it; *two years added to two years make four years* [italics mine]" (Stephens, 1911, p. 2).

"Require a fully-worded answer. The boy and the man had two legs, the dog four, so that though there were only three creatures there were eight legs" (Pridham, 1897, p. 114).

10. Questions should be changed around in a lively way to help fix the children's attention while giving them a love of mental arithmetic. Children may even give these types of exercises themselves.

" 'How many more tails than legs were there in the street?'
"Twist and turn your questions about; it produces great alertness and a sense of brightness . . . . Questions such as these will delight little ones, whereas if you said the same thing in a dull way you will produce stolid children. The little exercise just given involved addition, multiplication, analysis of number and subtraction, and might have been given so:—

Add 1 + 1 + 1
Multiply 3 x 2
How much is 4 more than 2.

The illustration given was either merely another way to exercise children in the four rules and not meant to be a direct translation of the preceding word problem or, perhaps, a typographical error was made in the original document.

"I will ask you to judge which method is suitable to a little child" (Pridham, 1897, pp. 114, 115).

"It is very important that the children should themselves set such exercises, not always the teacher. After a time the children are only too ready to do so. In fact I heard of one house where the parents, whose children had become very keen on the subject, positively had to forbid them setting arithmetical problems for their elders, or themselves at meal times; no doubt this was out of a very right and proper consideration for the digestive organs" (Pridham, 1897, p. 115).

11. Just as problems must remain within a child's comprehension, so must the vocabulary used. Introducing children to mathematical terms through engaging mental exercises will aid in their language acquisition and retention.

"In the initial stages of teaching Mental Arithmetic a good deal of language-teaching is necessary, for example such words as—single, double, both, couple, pair, half, brace, duet, twice, thrice, triplet, third, quarter, dozen, score, addition, subtraction, equal to, contained in, etc., all must be taught. These words will never be a puzzle to the children if they are introduced to them in some such way as this:—Two little boys were both given a ball, one had a red, the other a blue one. How many boys had a blue ball? How many boys had a red ball? How many boys had balls? If there were three children to have balls should we say they both are to have one? No. Why?

"One more example:—There was a woman once going to sell eggs at a market, and she counted them over and put them together in heaps of ten and twenty, and she called every big heap a score and every smaller one half-a-score. How many eggs had she in the big heaps, how many in the little? If she sold a score of eggs how many would this be? Suppose somebody wanted a dozen, how many less would that be than a score? Would half-a-score be more or less than a dozen?

"All words or terms needed for Mental Arithmetic must thus be made perfectly clear, in order that the children may have no difficulty with the material of their question. This is a subject in which a sure foundation, in all its branches, is of infinite importance" (Pridham, 1897, pp. 115, 116).

"After one or two such examples we begin sums involving shillings, and begin to use the term 'take away.' Take away 1*s*. 2*d*. from 5*s*. 8*d*., and what is left?" (Stephens, 1911, p. 8).

"If I had 8 oranges and gave away half of them, how many would that be? . . . If I had 9 and gave away one-third? What did giving away one-half mean? Dividing into 2 parts and giving away 1. What then do you think giving away one *third* would mean? Dividing into 3 equal parts and giving one away? Yes, so we divide 9 into 3 equal parts and give 1 away" (Stephens, 1911, p. 12).

12. Illustrative questions gradually give way to oral work with numbers and symbols involving one or more operations at a time.

"With this preparation it will no longer be necessary to be so graphic in your questions as you were to the little ones; gradually the questions may become severer, as the children begin to enjoy working simple problems for the satisfaction of their own mental activity. The four rules can now be taken with higher numbers—separately and then mixed. For example—

- \+   Think of 7 + 3 + 8 + 2 + 9 + 7 + 4 + 3 = 43.
    Think of ½ doz. + ½ of 18 + 1 + ¾ of a score + ¼ of a hundred = 56.
- \-   Think of 23 − 4 − 3 − 2 − 1 − 3 − 2 − 1 = 7.
- ×   Think of (2 × 2) + (2 × 3) + (2 × 4) + (2 × 5) = 28.
- /   Think of 24/2/3/2 = 2.

Think of 3 × 5 − ¼ of 20 + 10, double it + ½ of 6; how many people could have 7 units each = 6" (Pridham, 1897, p. 116).

13. Problems dealing with fractions and weights and measures are also worked orally before written work is given.

"Then one obtains from them the information that ⅕ of 20 equals 4 and 20 ÷ 5 = 4, so that ¼ of 20 means 20 ÷ 4, and one gives them a number of simple sums to be worked orally" (Stephens, 1911, pp. 12, 13).

"After the tables have been made the children read through them once or twice and then have a number of rapid oral questions. How many ounces in two pounds?

Notes

Reminder: Mental work should always be preceded by concrete lessons. See chapter 3 on manipulatives and chapter 2 on teaching Elementary Mathematics for more detail.

When presenting these problems orally, each step should be given by itself with a pause before moving on to the next. For example, the first problem would sound like "7+3," pause, "+8," pause, "+2," pause, etc. The length of the pause can be adjusted as the children grow more proficient.

"/" is used for the division symbol "÷" in this last example.

In 1 lb. 10 oz.? How many cwts. in 1 ton 6 cwt.? &c., &c., and then a large number of problems to be worked in their books" (Stephens, 1911, p. 13).

"I will not weary you with any more examples, but weights and measures should be treated in the same way" (Pridham, 1897, p. 117).

14. Children were led to discover for themselves methods for solving problems quickly.

"The children are taught to formulate rules for themselves by working out several examples from first principles, and when the rule *is* formulated to use it immediately to shorten their work, *e.g.*, a child works several sums such as, 'Find the cost of 12 things at 3*d.* each, 4*d.* each & &c.,' and hence formulates for himself the rule that 'the number of shillings per dozen is the same as the number of pence apiece,' this leads to the habit of investigation so essential to the higher mathematician" (Stephens, 1911, p. 18).

"We cannot in a consideration on the teaching of Mental Arithmetic neglect to notice those many devices given to us in all text-books on this subject for quick methods of working; perhaps the most familiar example of this is:—'To find the price of a dozen articles call the pence shillings and call every old farthing threepence.'

"I see no objection to such rules provided each child is skillfully led to discover them afresh for himself, otherwise they are not useful as a mental exercise, but thus treated they certainly are a great save of time in practical life" (Pridham, 1897, p. 118).

15. Additional examples used in oral work and mental arithmetic include Money and Marketing Sums, Dodging, and Unpicking.

> *There is no concrete evidence that "Unpicking" was used in Charlotte Mason's classrooms though it would seem to promote the power of attention and concentration.*

"A great many simple sums on money follow the experimental work, the numbers involved never exceeding 12; e.g., I bought three penny balls, two-pennyworth of toffee, and two two-penny balls of string. What change did the shopman give me out of a shilling? Or; I won a prize of 5*s.* and gave 2*d.* out of every shilling to my brother. How much did I give him?" (Stephens, 1911, p. 4).

"A boy had 2 florins.
He spent 3*d.* for a top
1*d.* " string
2*d.* " note-book
6*d.* " butterscotch
1*s.* " in the money-box;
had he anything left in his purse? 2*s.*

A man spent 7*s.* 6*d.* a week on rent,
How much a month? £1 10*s.*
How much a year? £18" (Pridham, 1897, p. 117).

"No modern teacher will, for a moment, think of teaching it by rote; but after the children have made up their own multiplication table, and discovered with joy that there are really only 36 answers practically in it, Dodging with the multiplication table is a good exercise, for it is necessary to have it at the top of the tongue" (Pridham, 1897, p. 118).

"A very favourite exercise and one requiring a good deal of steady concentration is what we call unpicking—

Think of 20 / 4 × 3 / 5 × 6 / 2 / 3. Answer; 3.
What had you before 3, 9; before 9, 18; before 18, 3; before 3, 15; before 15, 5; before 5, 20. When this is easy leave out 'before'—

Think of ¼ of 12 – ¼ of 8 + ¼ of 16 + ¼ of 20 = 10.
Now unpick. 10, 5, 1, 3.

"With a class of children it is very stimulating. To let each member join in giving part of a question, which shall be answered by the one whose turn comes last, thus making a chain of thought. Whenever I see signs of flagging attention I use this as a resource, and so far it has been unfailing" (Pridham, 1897, p. 118).

16. Numeration questions also lent themselves to oral and mental work.

"As well as questions on the four rules it will be found useful to give numeration questions to be done mentally. E.G.—

In 5,000 how many thousands?
Hundreds?
Fifties?
Twenty-fives?

How would you write down—
3,776? 3,076? 3,006? Etc." (Pridham, 1897, p. 118).

Questions to Ask Regarding Mental Arithmetic and Oral Work

- In the early years, is my child's work in arithmetic largely oral?
- Am I sure my child can *envision* a number of objects before advancing on to abstract numbers and symbols?
- Though my child may not yet be working out problems in figures, do I have him write out the answer on occasion to questions worked orally?
- Do I conclude my child's daily math lesson with five minutes of rapid mental work or have a scheduled time of Mental Arithmetic for my older children?
- When my child seems exceptionally alert, do I take the opportunity to exercise him with problems involving pure number?
- Am I sure to set oral problems within my child's comprehension?
- Do I require complete sentences when my child answers a word problem?
- Are the oral questions I give my child engaging?

Notes

An example of Dodging with the multiplication table would be "6 times what equals 35?; What number times 4 equals 24?; 5 fives are?"

Mental Arithmetic

Notes

- Do I allow my child to come up with mental exercises on his own or have him add on to questions I've given?
- Do I introduce and reinforce math vocabulary through the appealing use of mental work?
- As my child advances in understanding, is his mental work becoming more challenging, at times involving more than one mathematical operation?
- Am I allowing my child to discover shortcuts to mental work on his own?

Chapter 5
Geography

The Barry family sat around the dinner table in animated conversation. "So, didn't your homeschool group meet at the Wagner farm today?" Dad inquired.

Emily answered excitedly, "Oh, yes, we had such a nice time! We gathered eggs and fed apples to their horses. After that, Mrs. Wagner took us on a geography walk to a field that is lying fallow where we tried to judge its size by merely looking at it and then we paced it out. By the time we finished, the sun was high overhead so we had lunch under a giant oak, then drew the field to scale on paper."

"Dad," continued Lucas, "you would have loved it. Their farmyard is bound on the west side by a limestone bed creek and on the north by woods and another creek. It was so hot that we decided to go wading where the creeks join one another. Each ends in a small waterfall right before they meet up and one of the guys had the idea of finding out if one stream flows faster. Thomas Wagner grabbed a couple of 5-gallon buckets from the barn and we timed how fast each bucket filled at the cascades. We figured if we divided the size of the bucket by the number of seconds it took to fill we'd get a good estimate. For accuracy, we repeated the process a number of times to determine the average time it took to fill the bucket, then divided the bucket size by that."

"Well, it sounds like a fine day at the farm," answered Mr. Barry. As Emily and Lucas cleared the table, he turned to his wife, "The kids weren't very old when you began these geography walks and now just look at them . . . measuring distance, creating scale drawings, and determining volumetric flow!"

"I am grateful to Charlotte Mason," smiled Mrs. Barry. "In such an enjoyable way they learn about geography while their interest and understanding of math benefits as well."

Charlotte's Thoughts on Geography

1. Charlotte recognized that small things may teach great. Among these is what she termed Out-of-Door Geography, where children first met the wonders of their own vicinity.

"The child gets his rudimentary notions of geography as he gets his first notions of natural science, in those long hours out of doors of which we have already seen the importance" (Vol. 1, p. 273).

"It is probable that a child's vivid imagination puts him on a level with the mathematician in dealing with the planetary system, with the behaviour and character of Earth, with the causes of the seasons, and much besides" (Vol. 1, p. 278).

"There are certain ideas which children must get from within a walking radius of their own home if ever they are to have a real understanding of maps and of geographical terms" (Vol. 1, p. 73).

Geography

Notes

Charlotte Mason's own **Geographical Readers for Elementary Schools** *are an invaluable introduction to the study of geography. They are free for eReaders and are available in print through various suppliers.*

2. Geography walks, begun in the child's early years and continuing in school, were utilized in teaching elementary concepts in geography while also supporting a child's work in mathematics.

"All the work in Mathematics is greatly assisted by the 'geography' walks taken by the children, *i.e.*, walks during which exercises in pacing, in compass reading, in judging of heights and distances by eye are given; *e.g.*, 'make a plan of the road from our gate to the market square putting in telegraph poles, houses on the route, &c., &c.;' this is done by pacing the distances and taking directions with a pocket compass; or, 'find the amount of water per minute brought down by the stream above and below the water-works; hence find the amount of water taken by the works'; this would come in with the arithmetic lessons on cubic capacity" (Stephens, 1911, p. 17).

3. The idea of distance is gained on walks in the area surrounding a child's home.

"Distance is one of these, and the first idea of distance is to be attained by what children find a delightful operation. A child walks at his usual pace; somebody measures and tells him the length of his pace, and then he measures the paces of his brothers and sisters. Then such a walk, such a distance, here and there, is solemnly paced, and a little sum follows—so many inches or feet covered by each pace equals so many yards in the whole distance. Various short distances about the child's home should be measured in this way" (Vol. 1, p. 73).

4. Time as a means of measurement is another idea obtained during geography walks.

"And when the idea of covering distance is fully established, the idea of time as a means of measurement should be introduced. The time taken to pace a hundred yards should be noted down. Having found out that it takes two minutes to pace a hundred yards, children will be able for the next step—that if they have walked for thirty minutes, the walk should measure fifteen hundred yards; in thirty-five minutes they would have walked a mile, or rather seventeen hundred and fifty yards, and then they could add the ten yards more which would make a mile. The longer the legs the longer the pace, and most grown people can walk a mile in twenty minutes" (Vol. 1, pp. 73, 74).

5. Next, the idea of direction is to be introduced through the observation of the sun's course, its rising and setting, and the source of shadows and their properties.

"By the time they have got somewhat familiar with the idea of distance, that of *direction* should be introduced. The first step is to make children observant of the progress of the sun. The child who observes the sun for a year and notes down for himself, or dictates, the times of his rising and setting for the greater part of the year, and the points of his rising and setting, will have secured a basis for a good deal of definite knowledge. Such observation should take in the reflection of the sun's light, the evening light reflected by east windows, the morning light by west windows; the varying length and intensity of shadows, the cause of shadows, to be learned by the shadow cast by a figure between the blind and a candle. He should associate, too, the hot hours of the day with the sun high overhead, and the cool hours of the morning and evening with a low sun; and should be reminded, that if he stands straight before the fire, he feels the heat more than if he were in a corner of the room. When he is prepared by a little observation in the course of the sun, he is ready to take in the idea of direction, which depends entirely upon the sun" (Vol. 1, p. 74).

6. Once the idea of east and west are established through the rising and setting of the sun, the child will be able to tell in which direction objects and places lie by standing with his right hand to the east and his left to the west.

"Of course the first two ideas are that the sun rises in the east and sets in the west; from this fact he will be able to tell the direction in which the places near his own home, or the streets of his own town, lie. Bid him stand so that his right hand is towards the east where the sun rises, and his left towards the west where the sun sets. Then he is looking towards the north and his back is towards the south. All the houses, streets and towns on his right hand are to the east of him, those on the left are to the west. The places he must walk straight forward to reach are north of him, and the places behind him are to the south" (Vol. 1, pp. 74, 75).

7. The ability to determine directions in an unfamiliar place is the next discovery.

"If he is in a place new to him where he has never seen the sun rise or set and wants to know in what direction a certain road runs, he must notice in what direction his own shadow falls at twelve o'clock, because at noon the shadows of all objects fall towards the north. Then if he face the north, he has, as before, the south behind him, the east on his right hand, the west on his left; or if he face the sun at noon, he faces south" (Vol. 1, p. 75).

8. With a little practice, a child can now notice the directions of places and the direction of the wind.

"This will throw an interesting light for him on the names of our great railways. A child may become ready in noticing the directions of places by a little practice. Let him notice how each of the windows of his schoolroom faces, or the windows of each of the rooms in his home; the rows of houses he passes in his walks, and which are the north, south, east and west sides of the churches he knows. He will soon be prepared to notice the direction of the wind by noticing the smoke from the chimneys, the movement of branches, corn, grass, etc. If the wind blow from the north—'The north wind doth blow and we shall have snow.' If it blow from the west, a west wind, we expect rain. Care must be taken at this point to make it clear to the child that the wind is named after the quarter it comes from, and not from the point it blows towards—just as he is English because he was born in England, and not French because he goes to France" (Vol. 1, pp. 75, 76).

9. Now the ideas of distance and direction are combined, which produces a need for exactness of expression.

"The ideas of distance and direction may now be combined. Such a building is two hundred yards to the east of a gate, such a village two miles to the west. He will soon come across the difficulty, that a place is not exactly east or west, north or south. It is well to let him give, in a round-about way, the direction of places

Notes

The shadow will be cast toward the south at noon in the southern hemisphere.

Among the "great railways" of Charlotte's time were the Great Western Railway, the Great Eastern Railway, the Great Northern Railway, the North Eastern Railway, the London & South Western, and the South Eastern and Chatham Railway. A major achievement of Charlotte's era, the railways created a rail network of both safe and fast travel which linked London with the rest of Britain.

Notes

A mariner's compass is today commonly referred to as a magnetic compass, the instrument used for determining direction in relation to the earth's magnetic poles.

as—'more to the east than the west,' 'very near the east but not quite,' 'half-way between east and west.' He will value the exact means of expression all the more for having felt the need of them" (Vol. 1, p. 76).

10. Introducing the compass helps fine tune exact expression even more.

"Later, he should be introduced to the wonders of the mariner's compass, should have a little pocket compass of his own, and should observe the four cardinal and all the other points. These will afford him the names for directions that he has found it difficult to describe" (Vol. 1, p. 76).

11. Compass drill can be performed as specified by Charlotte Mason.

"Then he should do certain compass drill in this way: Bid him hold the N of the compass towards the north. 'Then, with the compass in your hand, turn towards the east, and you will see a remarkable thing. The little needle moves, too, but moves quite by itself in just the other direction. Turn to the west, and again the needle moves in the opposite direction to that in which you move. However little you turn, a little quiver of the needle follows your movement. And you look at it, wondering how the little thing could perceive you had moved, when you hardly knew it yourself. Walk straight on in any direction, and the needle is fairly steady; only fairly steady, because you are sure, without intending it, to move a little to the right or left. Turn round very slowly, a little bit at a time, beginning at the north and turning towards the east, and you may make the needle also move round in a circle. It moves in the opposite direction to yourself, for it is trying to get back to the north from which you are turning' " (Vol. 1, pp. 76, 77).

12. The idea of Boundaries is now gotten in degrees by first looking at what bounds a given space—such as a field, pond, or crop—and then drawing in the sand a simple plan of the examined space.

"The children having got the idea of direction, it will be quite easy to introduce that of boundaries—such and such a turnip field, for instance, is bounded by the highroad on the south, by a wheat crop on the south-east, a hedge on the north-east, and so on; the children getting by degrees the idea that the boundaries of a given space are simply whatever touches it on every side. Thus one crop may touch another without any dividing line, and therefore one crop bounds the other. It is well that children should get clear notions on this subject, or, later, they will be vague when they learn that such a county is 'bounded' by so and so. In connection with bounded spaces, whether they be villages, towns, ponds, fields, or what not, children should be led to notice the various crops raised in the district, why pasture-lands and why cornfields, what manner of rocks appear, and how many sorts of tree grow in the neighbourhood. For every field or other space that is examined, they should draw a rude plan in the sand, giving the shape roughly and lettering the directions as N, S, W, etc." (Vol. 1, p. 77).

13. Eventually the child will draw plans according to scale, first learning indoors, then pacing out a field and progressing to ground plans.

"By-and-by, when they have learned to draw plans indoors, they will occasionally pace the length of a field and draw their plan according to scale, allowing an inch for five or for ten yards. The ground-plans of garden, stables, house, etc., might follow" (Vol. 1, p. 77).

14. A child should be able to draw a rough plan of his local area, recognizing the locations of places and things and the distances between them.

"It is probable that a child's own neighbourhood will give him opportunities to learn the meaning of hill and dale, pool and brook, watershed, the current, bed, banks, tributaries of a brook, the relative positions of villages and towns; and all this local geography he must be able to figure roughly on a plan done with chalk on a rock, or with walking-stick in the gravel, perceiving the relative distances and situations of the places he marks" (Vol. 1, p. 78).

Questions to Ask about Outdoor Geography

- Do I utilize outdoor geography in our school?

Chapter 6
Geometry

"Today we start studying Geometry, Max," Teri exclaimed. "Do you know what *geometry* means? With a shake of her son's head, Teri continued, "Geometry is considered the art of measuring and the word comes from two Greek words—*ge* which means *the earth* or *land* and *metron* meaning *measure*. Do you remember the flooding of the Nile from when we read *Boy of the Pyramids?*"

"Sure, I really liked that book. When the water rose on the river, Kaffe and Sari were almost trapped. Each year the Nile overflowed and when the water receded, a rich layer of silt was left behind making the area around the river perfect for growing crops."

"Right, but those same floodwaters also washed away the boundary markers between the farmers' fields. It's believed that the Egyptians were the first to realize a formula for area measurement and used it to restore the boundaries washed away each year. This was among the duties of Egyptian priests, who also used area measurement to levy payment for their services. The more land a person owned, the more they would have to pay in taxes.

"We know that as early as 2900 B.C. geometry was also used by the Egyptians in building pyramids. The early Greeks brought geometry from Egypt to Greece around 600 B.C. and used it for building, astronomy, navigation, and laying out cities—some of the same things we use geometry for today. There are many different branches of geometry but the one we are going to learn about is called *plane* or *flat* geometry, because the properties we'll deal with can be drawn on paper or a *plane* or *flat* surface."

Max's mom handed him a cube he'd made out of stiff paper when he was younger, asking, "By looking at this cube, are you able to show me the *surface?*"

Max thought for a moment, "Well, the surface is the outer part which I can see and touch."

"Good, and what can you tell me about the surface of this rubber ball and the surface of your cube?"

Max thought a moment, "The surface of the ball is one piece but the surface on the cube isn't. The surface is in one, two, three, . . . six parts."

"We call each of the flat parts a *face*," said his mother. "Now, by looking at your cube how do the neighboring parts of the surface, or faces, meet?"

Running his finger across the edge, Max answered, "They meet in an edge or a line and those lines meet right here in points."

"Good. Go ahead and measure the cube then write down the measurements in your notebook. Be sure to put down the definitions you have so far for *surface*, *line*, and *points*. After that, we'll see what else we can find out about them."

Geometry in Charlotte's Classrooms

The study of geometry fell well within Charlotte's definition that "education is an atmosphere, a discipline, and a life." One would not find young children playing

Notes

The little Gradgrinds were the children of Thomas Gradgrind in Charles Dickens' 1854 serial novel, **Hard Times.** *In the novel, a measure of Dickens' satire was aimed at radical utilitarians in the character of Thomas Gradgrind, a rigid headmaster who believed children were empty vessels to be filled with facts. Gradgrind's own children received an education based in fact only. Nothing was allowed to ignite their imagination and their schoolroom was appropriately outfitted with this aim in mind.*

with geometrical forms or stitching geometrical patterns in Charlotte's classrooms. Her students would, however, get an idea of distance and direction through their hours spent out-of-doors. Habits of neatness and precision fostered through the children's work in paper modeling in their early years would be further cultivated in the drawing and measuring exercises found in Practical Geometry. As the children advanced, their work in geometry helped train them in forming correct judgments while cultivating an effort of mind and the power to reason logically.

Practical Geometry took place in Year 5 and Year 6 of Form II and was introduced through a short history of the subject and its practical uses. This was a weekly 30-minute lesson where children learned to handle mathematical tools, such as the compass and protractor and, through practical exercises in drawing and measurement, discovered for themselves foundational ideas in geometry. It was essential that the purpose of each exercise was apparent and Euclidian-like propositions were avoided.

In turn, Practical Geometry lent interest to the study of Formal Geometry. Simply called "Euclid" on the timetables, the study began in Year 7 and continued through the end of schooling. Through a short history, students were introduced to the leading thinkers of the science when presented with their corresponding theorems. For Years 7 and 8, Geometry was a 30-minute lesson, taking place each Friday with ten additional minutes on Saturday, perhaps to finish work begun the day before. Students also had 10 minutes of recitation of Euclidian proofs once a week. Geometry increased to two 30-minute lessons per week in Year 9 with the same schedule for those students who continued through Years 10, 11, and 12.

Geometry and the Early Years

1. Charlotte disdained an artificially prepared environment and did not fill her elementary classrooms with geometrical forms in an attempt to foster mathematical brilliance.

"In the 'forties' and 'fifties' it was currently held that the continual sight of the outward and visible signs (geometrical forms and figures) should beget the inward and spiritual grace of mathematical genius, or, at any rate, of an inclination to mathematics. But the educationalists of those days forgot, when they gave children boxes of 'form' and stuck up cubes, hexagons, pentagons, and what not, in every available schoolroom space, the immense capacity for being bored which is common to us all, and is far more strongly developed in children than in grown-up people. The objects which bore us, or the persons who bore us, appear to wear a bald place in the mind, and thought turns from them with sick aversion. Dickens showed us the pathos of it in the schoolroom of the little Gradgrinds, which was bountifully supplied with objects of uncompromising outline. Ruskin, more genially, exposes the fallacy. No doubt geometric forms abound,—the skeletons of which living beauty, in contour and gesture, in hill and plant, is the covering; and the skeleton is beautiful and wonderful to the mind which has already entered within the portals of geometry. But children should not be presented with the skeleton, but with the living forms which clothe it" (Vol. 1, p. 263).

"Besides, is it not an inverse method to familiarise the child's eye with patterns made by his compasses, or stitched upon his card, in the hope that the form will beget the idea? For the novice, it is probably the rule that the idea must beget the form, and any suggestion of an idea from a form comes only to the initiated. I do not think that any direct preparation for mathematics is desirable. The child, who has been allowed to think and not compelled to cram, hails the new study with delight when the due time for it arrives. The reason why mathematics are a great study is because there exists in the normal mind an affinity and capacity for this study; and too great an elaboration, whether of teaching or of preparation, has, I think, a tendency to take the edge off this manner of intellectual interest" (Vol. 1, pp. 263, 264).

2. Though there was no formal preparation for mathematics, the dexterity and neatness children gained in handicrafts would help them in their future study of geometry.

"During his sixth and seventh years spent in Class I., he has learnt how to work in carton; to model cubes and chairs and many other things; each model involving the drawing of straight lines of given lengths, the keeping of square corners, and very neat and accurate cutting out. All this serves him in good stead now, his fingers can hold a ruler steady and straight, he draws neat and tidy lines, and is accurate" (Stephens, 1911, p. 14).

Carton Work and Paper Modeling in Charlotte's Classrooms

Grades 1–3

In the earlier years of the Parents' Union School, all three classes of Form I, approximately our first through third grades, worked from *Carton Work* by G. C. Hewitt. They made useful items, such as pen trays, salt cellars, and match boxes and made models of larger objects, such as a table.

Grade 1

Six and seven-year-olds used the book *Paper Folding* by H. G. Paterson. They made between eight and eleven models per term from the book, along with two original models per term "along the same lines."

Grades 2 and 3

Students in Form IA, approximately our second and third grades, worked through a series titled *Paper Modelling* by M. Swannell, completing five models per term.

3. The study of geography, begun in the early years, also supported the children's work in geometry.

"All the work in Mathematics is greatly assisted by the 'geography' walks taken

Notes

Information taken from PNEU programmes between 1908 and 1923.

Geometry

Notes

See chapter 5 on Geography for a more thorough examination of the relationship between the subjects of geography and mathematics in a Charlotte Mason education.

Stephens is quoting from John Ruskin's Mornings in Florence, being simple studies of Christian Art for English Travellers. *London: George Allen, 1894. p. 134.*

Year 5 was the lower form of Class IIA in Form II—our approximate grade 5, ages 10 and 11. Year 7, Class IIIB in Form III, is approximately our grade 7, ages 12 and 13.

by the children, *i.e.*, walks during which exercises in pacing, in compass reading, in judging of heights and distances by eye are given; *e.g.*, 'make a plan of the road from our gate to the market square putting in telegraph poles, houses on the route, &c., &c.'; this is done by pacing the distances and taking directions with a pocket compass; or, 'find the amount of water per minute brought down by the stream above and below the water-works; hence find the amount of water taken by the works'; this would come in with the arithmetic lessons on cubic capacity" (Stephens, 1911, p. 17).

4. The truth and beauty of geometry was saluted as well.

"To use Ruskin's words, anent Geometry: 'You have now learned, young ladies and gentlemen, to read, to speak, to think, to sing, and to see . . . Here is your carpenter's square for you, and you may safely and wisely contemplate the ground a little, and the measures and laws relating to that, seeing you have got to abide upon it:— and have properly looked at the stars; not before then, lest, had you studied the ground first, you might perchance never have raised your heads from it. Geometry is here considered as the arbitress of all laws of practical labour, issuing in beauty' " (Stephens, 1911, pp. 14, 15).

Practical Geometry, also called Concrete or Experimental Geometry

1. In Year 5 children began lessons in Practical Geometry, gaining physical habits and foundational ideas before embarking on the formal study of geometry in Year 7.

"During the last year he has begun Geometry, taking the subject quite experimentally and practically, learning how to handle the instruments, to use his eye as a judge of lengths and areas, to know the names and some properties of certain geometrical forms, *e.g.*, he discovers by drawing and measurement facts about the intersection of the diagonals of a square and a rectangle, and of parallelograms in general, and the meanings of some geometrical terms, *e.g.*, bisect, perpendiculars, &c., so that when the study of the subject is properly begun he starts with a certain equipment, the foundational ideas are mastered to some extent, and he is able to concentrate his attention on the reasoning out of propositions" (Stephens, 1911, p. 14).

2. Beginning with points and lines, problems are presented in such a way that children are able to obtain facts and determine definitions themselves.

"The Geometry lessons begin with points, and with lines, straight and curved, the children's own definitions being taken if possible; problems are given them which will elicit certain facts about lines, *e.g.*, 'draw as many straight lines as you can through a certain point,' or 'take 3 points and join each one to every other, how many lines have you?' " (Stephens, 1911, p. 15).

3. Practice in judging lengths of lines using concrete objects is also given.

"We also give a lot of practice in judging of the lengths of lines both in centimetres and inches, the amount of error always being found; it is all done of course by work on the concrete, the schoolroom and things out of doors provide an endless supply of straight lines" (Stephens, 1911, p. 15).

4. Children learn the meaning of bisect *and* trisect, *attempting to divide lines into equal halves and thirds without the use of a ruler.*

"We learn the meaning of 'bisect' and 'trisect,' and try to perform these operations without measurement" (Stephens, 1911, p. 15).

5. Plans to Scale—Scale is studied next by exercises in drawing to scale and the investigation of maps.

"The next step is to draw plans to scale. I want to draw a picture of the window on a piece of paper not nearly large enough. How shall I do it? Why, draw it smaller, of course. how much smaller? This invites suggestions of which the best should be taken. Eight times as small? Very well, but how shall I be sure that it is eight times as small? measure it. How? Measure each side and make each eight times as small. This is done and the window drawn and divided into its component panes, the scale of course is very carefully put in. After this doors, books, &c., are drawn to scale, a plan of the schoolroom made with windows, doors, and fireplace in. Then we get out our atlases and see that all maps are really plans drawn to scale, and we can find out by measuring and using the scale how far places are from each other, though here we must go carefully, as the scale given on a map is not by any means accurate. The scale on all maps must necessarily differ in different directions, and the results obtained can therefore be only approximate, though sufficiently so to be of use and interest to the children" (Stephens, 1911, p. 15).

6. Interesting problems are given in which the children draw plans to scale to determine the distance between two objects.

"After practice in map-measuring, we have a few problems, such as:—'If I look west from my house, I see a lighthouse 4 miles away, if I look west I see a church spire 3 miles away. Draw a plan (scale 1 mile to 1 inch), and find out how far the lighthouse is from the tower' " (Stephens, 1911, p. 15).

7. The Circle—Children draw circles, learn the meanings of related terms, and work out interesting problems in connection with their previous work.

"The circle comes next, the children practise drawing them, and learn the meaning of radius, centre, circumference, arc, chord, diameter; then they draw circles, concentric, intersecting, &c., &c., and have problems connecting circles and their former work, *e.g.*, a lighthouse whose light has a radius of 4 ½ miles, is 32 miles from another light, with a radius of 3 miles. Draw a plan to find what space of darkness a ship would have to cross in going from one to the other" (Stephens, 1911, p. 15).

8. Angles—The formation of angles, their names, and magnitudes are studied next.

"Angles are taken next, and are generally defined as 'corners' by the children, they see the 2 ways in which a 'corner' may be formed; by 2 lines meeting or by

> **Notes**
>
> *The compass referred to here is not the magnetic compass used in geography, but the drawing compass, with a point at the end of one leg and a pencil at the end of the other, that helps one draw accurate circles and curves.*

1 line revolving about another; they also learn that blunt and sharp angles are called obtuse and acute, and what a right angle is like. They also find out how the magnitude of an angle can be tested, and that it is not affected by the length of its arms, for two equal angles can be formed by the opening out of a large and a small pair of compasses, for instance" (Stephens, 1911, p. 16).

9. Children then learn the use of the protractor.

"The use of the protractor comes next, and when the children are proficient in this, they can find out the properties of vertically opposite angles, angles in a circle, &c., by drawing and measuring for themselves. The clock-face provides useful practice in the magnitudes of angles and in drawing circles" (Stephens, 1911, p. 16).

10. All questions must serve a purpose so as not to leave a child with an incomplete idea.

"Plans are given involving the measuring of angles and distances. The questions must all have some purpose in them; a question like 'Draw XY 4 inches long, at X draw a line making an angle 58° with XY, and at Y a line making an angle *[sic]* an angle 48° with XY,' leaves an unfinished idea in the child's mind and makes his geometry lesson a play at purposeless line and angles; or makes his work machine-like; he stops like a machine at the drawing of that third line because he sees no reason for stopping there; and he is ready like a machine for the next such pointless demand" (Stephens, 1911, p. 16).

> *The child doesn't stop because he sees the reason or purpose for stopping, but rather, the child stops like a machine and starts like a machine.*

11. Direction is then added to the problems.

"After angles, we are able to take the 16 points of the compass, with many exercises from maps or from plans which the children draw" (Stephens, 1911, p. 16).

12. Work on parallels easily follows the work with direction.

"Work on parallels follows very easily from this; as parallel lines are simply those in the same direction, *e.g.*, railway lines, or roads in the neighbourhood; it can be ocularly demonstrated that two people walking always in the same direction and apart, never draw any nearer each other" (Stephens, 1911, p. 16).

13. Familiarizing children with alternate, exterior, and interior angles prevents confusion in their future work with propositions.

"The names of the angles 'alternate,' 'exterior,' and 'interior,' are learnt: this is really advisable as an aid to the future when the proposition dealing with parallel lines is taken. If the pupils are not already familiar with the names of the angles formed by a pair of parallel lines with a transversal, we find that the proposition involving the properties of these angles invariably proves a source of confusion and difficulty" (Stephens, 1911, p. 16).

14. The introduction of set squares is next.

"The children are next introduced to set squares, and shown how to use them, and are taught how to draw parallel lines in this way" (Stephens, 1911, p. 16).

> *Set squares are called triangles in American English.*

15. During this time Euclidian-style propositions are to be avoided. All the work is practical, laying the groundwork for reasoning out propositions in the future.

"Throughout this early part of the work we try to avoid as far as possible any approach to a proposition in the style of Euclid; all the work is a preparation for the logical proving of propositions that is to come; and any approach to it now is apt to result in some of the parrot-work so much affected by former students of Euclid. All we teach them, therefore, at this stage is to bisect a straight line (this being a very simple proposition can be taken as one of the ways in which circles may be used), and perhaps to bisect an angle and make one angle equal to another, though, as these latter mean necessarily a mechanical effort of memory, it is advisable to omit them with a slow class" (Stephens, 1911, pp. 16, 17).

16. Absolute accuracy is required.

"Throughout the work *accuracy* in all measurements and drawings is insisted upon, as this is absolutely necessary when so much is done visually" (Stephens, 1911, p. 17).

17. The study of Practical Geometry develops the physical and mental habits important for the further study of mathematics while providing the foundational ideas to be developed in Formal Geometry.

"After a year of geometry the children have obtained a good idea of direction and distance, some familiarity with ordinary mathematical instruments, habits of neatness and accuracy which are of value in one's dealings with later Mathematics, and some small power of logical reasoning acquired by the tackling of the problems presented" (Stephens, 1911, p. 17).

"Geometry trains the mind to severe reasoning, the hand to absolute accuracy, and it lies at the root base of many important and honourable professions, which is a real though utilitarian reason why we should teach it. The child begins to learn geometrical truths when he finds out that the top of the table is a flat thing with edges (a plain surface) and that the parallel hedges of the high road do not meet together in the far distance" (Pennethorne, 1899, p. 549).

Formal Geometry

The study of Formal Geometry was begun in Year 7 and continued through the end of a student's schooling. For Years 7 and 8, Geometry was a 30-minute lesson taking place each Friday. There was an additional ten-minute lesson on Saturday, which may have been used to finish work begun the day before. Students in these years also had 10 minutes of repetition of Euclidian proofs once a week. Geometry increased to two 30-minute lessons per week in Year 9 with the same schedule for those students who continued through Years 10, 11, and 12.

A look at the geometry books used in Charlotte's schools during her lifetime reveals that after students examined propositions and theorems they would then apply their knowledge in practical exercises, with deductive exercises continuing

Notes

Quotes cited Pennethorne refer to Pennethorne, R. A., "P.N.E.U. Principles As Illustrated by Teaching," The Parents' Review, Volume 10 (1899): p. 549, http://www.amblesideonline.org/PR/PR10p549PNEUPrinciplesIllustrated.shtml.

Notes

alongside practical exercises throughout, thus ensuring a living treatment of the subject.

1. First lessons in Formal Geometry are expansions of students' earlier study of Practical Geometry.

"It is on this common and already existing knowledge [the top of the table is a flat thing with edges (a plain surface) and that the parallel hedges of the high road do not meet together in the far distance] on which we must base our first lessons on geometrical definitions and axioms" (Pennethorne, 1899, p. 549).

2. The idea of each proposition studied is kept in the forefront as the students discover its logical and obvious proof through construction and reasoning.

"Geometry is especially remarkable in that it converts each idea it gives into a habit of mind or action in construction, and a base for the next idea to rise upon. Thus when we give a lesson upon a proposition we make clear the idea (equality perhaps of two triangles) to be conveyed, and then we help the pupil to discover the logical as well as the obvious proof of its reality, and never make the children learn by heart without comprehension a chatter of ABC=Q.E.D." (Pennethorne, 1899, p. 549).

3. The child is exercised in each geometrical truth before proceeding to the next.

"Having gone over with the pupil the method of reasoning, we ensure that it shall become habitual by giving exercises (riders) on that particular truth before proceeding to the next" (Pennethorne, 1899, p. 549).

4. The ability to prove things geometrically helps the student appreciate abstract thinking.

"Nothing can help children better to understand that abstract logical reasoning is not unreal than the mental discipline of going from figure to proof and proof to figure in what we term 'propositions' " (Pennethorne, 1899, p. 549).

5. Students should be introduced to the leading thinkers of geometry when presented with their corresponding theorems.

"How interesting arithmetic and geometry might be if we gave a short history of their principal theorems; if the child were mentally present at the labours of a Pythagoras, a Plato, a Euclid, or in modern times, of a Viete, a Descartes, a Pascal, or a Leibnitz" (Vol. 2, p. 128).

Charlotte quotes French philosopher Alfred Fouillé regarding an education of ideas.

"How living would Geometry become in the light of the discoveries of Euclid as he made them!" (Vol. 6, p. 233).

A Sample Lesson in Geometry

In Volume 14 of *The Parents' Review*, Charlotte introduced a feature to the monthly periodical called "Notes of Lessons," which provided an illustration of children's regular studies.

"We have thought that it might be of use to our readers (in their own families) to publish from month to month during the current year, Notes of Lessons prepared by students of the House of Education for the pupils of the Practising School. We should like to say, however, that such a Lesson is never given as a *tour de force*, but is always an illustration or an expansion of some part of the children's regular studies (in the Parents' Review School), some passage in one or other of their school books. —ED."

Notes of Lessons
Volume 14, 1903, pgs. 544–548

II. Subject: Geometry
Group: Mathematics. Class II Average age, 10. Time: 30 minutes
by W. T. Wilkinson.
Objects.
　To teach the pupils to reason inductively.
　To cultivate the inventive powers and encourage self-reliance.
　To train the hand in neatness and the eye in precision.
　To train the pupils in a habit of forming correct judgments.
　To introduce the pupils to a new subject, viz., geometry.

First, a short definition and history of geometry is given.

Step I.—Find out if the pupils know that the word "geometry" means the measurement of the earth, and is derived from two Greek words—*ge* = the earth, and *metron* = a measure.

Give a brief sketch of the history of geometry as far as it is known. It is supposed to have been invented by the Egyptians when they wanted to restore their landmarks effaced by the inundations of the Nile. Later they used it for measuring such things as areas, solids, etc.; we know that this was in 1700 BC., because of a papyrus preserved in the British Museum. The ancient Greeks used geometry a great deal, but for them it meant the measurement of surfaces, corners, etc.

In the time of Roman power it was not used, but was revived again in the 17th century, and adopted in England and France, and has been used ever since.

Next, children give any practical uses of geometry with which they are familiar and then are told about the branch of geometry they are to study.

Step II.—Find out if the pupils know some of the uses to which geometry is put, e.g., to find out the distances of the heavenly bodies from the earth, to measure from place to place when both places are inaccessible, to measure the surface of the earth, fields, etc., etc. Tell the pupils that there are many different branches of geometry, and the one about which they are going to learn is called "plane" or "flat" geometry, because the things treated of can be drawn on paper.

Through observation and measurement, children define *surface, line*, and *point* themselves and write their measurements and definitions neatly in a notebook.

Step III.—Give the pupils a cube and let them find out for themselves, by observation and measurement, the definitions of a surface, a straight line, and a

Notes

Taken from Wilkinson, W. T., "Notes of Lessons," The Parents' Review, *Volume 14 (1903): pp. 544–48,* http://www.amblesideonline.org/PR/PR14p544NotesofLessons.shtml.

Notes

point. Let the measurements be put down neatly in a book and the corresponding definitions written in beside them.

Children discover for themselves the three kinds of lines which can be drawn between two points by drawing on a chalkboard and then provide examples of each via roads, etc.

Step IV.—Put two dots on the board to represent points, and let the pupils find out the three kinds of lines that can be drawn between them, viz., straight, curved and zigzag, and that the straight line is the shortest distance between the two points. Let the pupils illustrate these three lines by reference to roads, etc.

Using matchsticks, children explore the different ways lines either meet or do not meet and diagram these in their notebooks.

Step V.—As the pupils know that a straight line has no breadth or thickness, give them each two matches, and let them put these in as many different positions with relation to each other as they can: (1) meeting with four, two, and one corners or angles respectively; and (2) not meeting; (a) where the two lines would meet if lengthened or produced, and (b) where they would never meet. Let diagrams of these be put neatly into the book.

Using their diagrams, children define *angle* and *parallel lines*, then give examples of each using various objects.

Step VI.—Let the pupils give the definitions of an angle and parallel lines from their drawings, and illustrate them from the cube and numerous other objects, such as the corners of the room, of the table, railway lines, the sides of a room, a picture, etc.

As a form of review, the children again provide definitions and examples of terms previously covered.

Step VII.—Recapitulate by asking for definitions and illustrations of a surface, a line, a point, a straight line, an angle and parallel lines.

Mathematical Instruments

According to PNEU programmes, childrens' work in geometry would require the following mathematical instruments:
- A flat ruler, one edge being graduated in centimeters and millimeters, the other in inches and tenths
- Two set squares (called *triangles* in American English); one with angles of 45°, and the other with angles of 60° and 30°
- A pair of pencil compasses
- A pair of dividers calipers
- A semi-circular protractor
- Tracing paper and squared paper (what we refer to as *graph* or *grid paper*)

Questions to Ask about Geometry

Grades 1-4
- Are those handicrafts that beget dexterity and neatness—such as paper folding and paper modeling—a part of my child's generous curriculum?
- Am I sure to include skills such as compass reading and pacing in my child's study of geography?

Grades 5, 6
- Are we making Practical Geometry part of our generous curriculum?
- Is my child's study of geometry at this point hands-on and experimental?
- Are problems presented in such a way that my child is able to obtain geometrical facts and determine definitions for himself?
- Is my child doing exercises in both standard and metric measurement?
- Is my child gaining skill in the use of mathematical instruments?
- Do the exercises serve a clear purpose to my child so as not to give him the idea that the study of geometry is pointless?
- Am I sure to avoid Euclidian-style propositions at this time?
- Do I require absolute accuracy of my child?

Grades 7 – 12
- Are my child's first lessons in Formal Geometry based on commonplace knowledge?
- Is the idea behind each proposition clear to my child as he discovers the proof through step-by-step construction and reasoning?
- Am I sure to introduce to my child the leading thinkers of geometry when they are presented with their corresponding theorems?

Notes

Geometry Scope and Sequence

The charts below outline which topics of geometry were taught in which grades in Charlotte's schools. (Rendered from PNEU programmes used up until 1923 and available at time of publication.)

Approximate U.S. Grade	5	6
Approximate Age	10–11	11–12
Practical Geometry		
History	x	
Solids, Surfaces and Lines	x	x
Measurement of Straight Lines	x	
Plans to Scale	x	
Circles	x	
Angles	x	
Construction of Angles with Ruler and Compass	x	
Using a Protractor	x	
Bisecting Angles	x	
Direction	x	
Parallels	x	
Perpendiculars	x	x
Triangles		x
Congruence of Triangles - Practical		x
Quadrilaterals		x
Areas		x
Misc. Constructions, Circles, Regular Polygons		x

Approximate U.S. Grade	7	8	9–12
Approximate U.S. Age	12–13	13–14	14–18
Geometry			
Axioms, Definitions, Postulates	x		
Lines and Angles	x	x	x
Triangles	x		x
Parallelograms	x		
Triangles			
Exterior and Interior Angles	x	x	
Inequalities	x	x	
Parallels			
Parallels Demonstrated by Rotation	x		
Angles of a Triangle	x		x
Angles of Rectilinear Figures	x		
Congruent Triangles	x		
Parallelograms	x	x	x
Diagonal Scales	x		
Linear Measurements	x		
Problems on Lines and Angles	x		x
Construction of Triangles	x		x
Identical Equality of Triangles	x	x	
Exercises on Parallels and Parallelograms	x	x	
Practical Geometry			
Problems on Lines and Angles		x	
Construction of Triangles		x	x
Construction of Quadrilaterals		x	x
Loci		x	x
Intersection of Loci		x	x
Loci		x	
Concurrence of Straight Lines in a Triangle		x	x
Areas			
Definitions		x	x
Area of a Rectangle		x	x
Area of a Parallelogram		x	x
Area of a Triangle		x	x
Area of a Trapezium		x	
Area of any Quadrilateral		x	
Area of any Rectilineal Figures		x	
Pythagorean Theorem		x	
Experimental Proofs of Pythagorean Theorem		x	
Problems of Areas		x	
Axes of Reference. Coordinates.			x
The Circle			
Definitions and First Principles			x
Symmetry. Symmetrical Properties of Circles			x
Chords			x
Angles in a Circle			x
Tangency			
Definitions and First Principles			x
Review Circle, Chords and Angles in a Circle			x

Note: Either Introduction or Review with more difficult examples taken

Chapter 7
Algebra

Mary, Heidi, and Sherri were busy in the kitchen preparing food for their local church's weekly soup dinner when the conversation turned to the home education of their older children.

"I was one of those kids that sat in Algebra class asking, 'Why do we need to study this anyway?' " revealed Heidi. "What if my children ask me and I can't give them the satisfactory answer I so longed for at their age?"

Mary responded with encouragement, "Heidi, we can't forget what we've learned regarding Charlotte Mason's philosophy of education. First and foremost, algebra is important because its study increases a student's power of attention and reasoning while also fostering the habit of accuracy. Algebra is the generalization of the ideas found in arithmetic, making it a God-given tool of practical use. By seeking the value of an unknown we are able to solve problems we face in everyday life."

Sherri chimed in, "For example, we use algebra all the time in this kitchen. When we first started offering dinner, we prepared our recipes to serve 60 people. Since then our turnout has grown weekly, requiring constant modification of our recipes. Sometimes the recipes and numbers are easier to work with and we don't seem to give it much thought; however, where ratios need to be exact or we're following a strict budget, we set up a simple algebraic equation to decide the quantity of each ingredient we'll need."

"Hey, that's exactly what I did today to determine how much rice and water I should use to feed tonight's crowd," exclaimed Heidi.

"Precisely, and now you've got the answer to your initial question," Sherri replied. "Whether we need to modify a recipe, calculate how much wood is needed to build bookshelves in the family room, or figure out what time we should leave home to make it to the Shakespeare play on time, algebra is part of our daily lives."

"So using algebraic terminology, one could say Heidi is 'solving proportions using cross multiplication'," Mary quipped; "but instead, we simply call it 'not serving gooey rice.' "

Algebra in Charlotte's Classrooms

Charlotte Mason tells us that *every* subject can be approached in a living way, and algebra is no exception. At about the age of twelve, or seventh grade, Elementary Algebra was introduced to students in a way that would kindle their interest in the new subject.

Beginning with a short history of algebra given by the teacher, children were next asked for the different signs of operations used in arithmetic, giving the definitions themselves. Through this review, the use of symbols seemed to arise naturally from arithmetic as children crossed the border into algebra with the consideration of negative numbers and the idea of letters standing for *any* number. The discipline of good habits was equally present as accuracy was encouraged, and their power

Notes

Information compiled from PNEU Programmes and Examinations, http://www.amblesideonline.org/library.shtml#pneuprogrammes and Charlotte Mason Digital Collection, http://www.redeemer.ca/charlotte-mason.

The textbook cited is Hall, H. S. A School Algebra. c.1911. 1962 reprint. London: Macmillan, 1911. i.456. http://www.hathitrust.org.

of concentration increased in the working out of examples in the simpler rules of algebra.

According to timetables and programmes from Charlotte's schools, in about ninth grade the formal study of Algebra took the place of Arithmetic on Wednesdays in one 30-minute lesson. In grades 10–12, more advanced Algebra was added and lessons increased to two 30-minute lessons per week with no homework given through the entire course of study.

Though Charlotte herself wrote little regarding algebra in comparison to other subjects, an inspection of the textbook used and the sequence of its study found in school programmes reflects an adherence to her philosophy of education, with no less careful consideration and graduation in its teaching. During the first year of formal study, students mastered rules using easier types of equations while keeping the object in view—that is, seeking the value of the unknown—always before them. Examples would be worked orally as well as written. In order to secure neatness and orderly arrangement, simpler equations involving little work were employed in the beginning stages of study.

As the study of algebra advanced with each school year, rules were reviewed and more complex examples were taken from the textbook. Looking at the work set in Charlotte's programmes, it is evident that the PNEU chartered its own course, diverging from the order of the textbook or even encouraging members to simply continue where they had left off—a further example that, in a Mason education, we teach the child, not the textbook.

Charlotte's Words

1. The obvious practical value of higher mathematics does not outweigh its direct use in training mental and moral habits.

"The practical value of arithmetic to persons in every class of life goes without remark. But the use of the study in practical life is the least of its uses. The chief value of arithmetic, like that of the higher mathematics, lies in the training it affords to the reasoning powers, and in the habits of insight, readiness, accuracy, intellectual truthfulness it engenders" (Vol. 1, p. 254).

2. In the appendices of School Education, *Charlotte gives an outline of her students' work to persuade educators considering the use of an* Education by Books *in their own public or private schools, with Elementary Algebra introduced around seventh and eighth grade and more advanced Algebra in grades 9–12.*

"The six years' work—from six to twelve—which I suggest, should and does result in the power of the pupils…

"(h) [They] Should have a knowledge of Elementary Algebra, and should have done practical exercises in Geometry" (Vol. 3, p. 301).

"Girls are usually in Class IV for two or three years, from fourteen or fifteen to seventeen, after which they are ready to specialise and usually do well. The programme for Class IV is especially interesting; it adds Geology and Astronomy to the sciences studied, more advanced Algebra to the Mathematics, and sets the history of Modern Europe instead of French history" (Vol. 3, p. 294).

A Sample Lesson in Algebra

In Volume 14 of *The Parents' Review*, Charlotte introduces a feature to the monthly periodical called "Notes of Lessons" which, written by student teachers, serves as an illustration of children's regular studies.

"We have thought that it might be of use to our readers (in their own families) to publish from month to month during the current year, Notes of Lessons prepared by students of the House of Education for the pupils of the Practising School. We should like to say, however, that such a Lesson is never given as a *tour de force*, but is always an illustration or an expansion of some part of the children's regular studies (in the Parents' Review School), some passage in one or other of their school books. —ED."

Notes of Lessons.
Volume 14, 1903, pgs. 382–388

II. Subject: Algebra.
Group: Mathematics. Class III. Average age, 12. Time: 30 minutes.
by H. M. A. Bell.
Objects.
    To introduce a new branch of mathematics, touching on the two first simple rules.
    To increase the power of attention and reasoning.
    To encourage accuracy.
    To stimulate interest in a new subject.

First, a short history of algebra is given.

Step I.—Tell the children about the introduction of algebra: Arabs derived it from the Hindus, and it was from Arabs that Europeans first obtained their acquaintance with it. The first books on algebra were written in the fourth century. Algebra derived its name through the Italian and Spanish from the Arabic Al-jebr=the resetting of anything broken, hence combination, i.e., the combination of numbers and quantities. Algebra, the science or knowledge of numbers, of later growth than arithmetic, was at first merely a kind of universal arithmetic, symbols taking the place of numbers. It is now a distinct branch of mathematics.

Next, signs of operations and their use are reviewed.

Step II.—Ask the children for the different signs used in arithmetic and for their respective values, as:—

Equals, = stands for "is equal to" or "are equal to"; example, 3 + 2 = 5.

Plus, + put before a number means that what that symbol represents has to be added; as, 4 + 5 = 9. (Ask for examples of symbols with + between.)

Minus, - put before a number means that what that symbol represents has to be subtracted; as, 5 - 2 = 3. (Ask for examples of symbols with - between.)

When a symbol has neither + nor - written before it, + is always understood.

Discuss positive and negative signs and numbers, showing from examples

> *Taken from Bell, H. M. A., "Notes of Lessons," The Parents' Review, Volume 14 (1903): pp. 382–88, http://www.amblesideonline.org/PR/PR14p382Lessons.shtml.*

Algebra

Notes

using negative numbers how we leave the boundary of arithmetic and enter into algebra.

Step III.—Shew the difference between positive and negative signs, and how they are used, the positive before a positive number or one to be added, the negative before a negative number or one to be subtracted. All numbers are either positive or negative. (Ask for examples of each kind.) Shew from examples how, in considering negative numbers, we overstep the boundary of arithmetic and enter on algebra. Thus in arithmetic you cannot subtract 7 from 4 to give a sensible answer, but in algebra you can have negative answers.

Interesting story problems using negative numbers are worked.

Step IV.—Let the children work the following examples:—

1. A man, starting from a sign-post, walks on for 7 steps (positive) and then goes back 10 steps (negative) to pick up something. How far would he be from the post?
2. A boy gained 16 marks and lost 18. How many did he gain on the whole?
3. A owes B 6 pounds, and B owes A 8 pounds. How much does A owe B on the whole?
4. A cart was driven 15 miles along a road running south, the driver turned the horses round and drove 20 miles back. How far south was it then?
5. A boy had gone already 20 steps towards his school when he found that he had forgotten to buy a book at a shop which was 26 steps in the opposite direction. When he was at the shop how much nearer school was he than when he started?

Via questions and examples introduce the idea of letters standing for any number in algebra and how this differs from arithmetic where a digit has a single, definite value. Children then work examples to find the unknown.

Step V.—Ask the children if they know how algebra differs from arithmetic, i.e., that in algebra we use letters as well as numbers, and any letter may stand for any number. Thus a may = 1, 2, 3, 24, etc., and any other letter may have the same value. Give the following examples to be worked out:—

1. If $a = 3$, $b = 6$, and $c = 2$, find the value of:—
    (1) $a + 4$
    (2) $b - 3$
    (3) $c - 5$
    (4) $a + b - c$
2. If $x = 6$
    (1) What is half x?
    (2) What is $1/3$ of x?
3. If $x = 12$
    (1) What is twice x?
    (2) What is six times x?
4. I have x pounds, you have y pounds, and someone else has z pounds. How many have we altogether?
5. How old are you now? How old will you be in x years?
6. If you are 15 years old now, how old were you v years ago?
7. Add together p, q, x, a, b.
8. Subtract a and b from x.

Questions to Ask about Algebra

- Am I sure to kindle my child's interest in algebra by introducing the subject through a short, interesting history?
- Do I (or does the textbook) introduce the practical side of algebra as early as possible?
- Am I allowing my child to proceed in a slow, steady manner, mastering rules in equations before moving on?
- Do I insist upon neatness and orderly arrangement throughout my child's work?
- Does my child receive plenty of review before moving on to more complex work?

Notes

Algebra

Algebra Scope and Sequence

The charts below outline which topics of algebra were taught in which grades in Charlotte's classrooms. (Rendered from PNEU programmes used up until 1923 and available at time of publication.)

Approximate U.S. Grade	7–8
Approximate U.S. Age	12–14
Introduction to Elementary Algebra	
History	x
Signs of Operation in Arithmetic	x
Negative Numbers	x
Symbols	x
Unknown Values	x
Brackets	x

Note: Pre-algebra was not a term found in Charlotte's writings but the modern understanding of Pre-algebra was taught in her schools. Basically, Pre-algebra is everything upon which the concepts of algebra are built. When we see standard mathematical operations, fractions, decimals and their conversions taught in Arithmetic, we are seeing what we term Pre-algebra.

See the Arithmetic Scope and Sequence charts found in chapter 2.

Approximate U.S. Grade	9–12
Approximate Age	14–18
Algebra	
General Arithmetic, Symbols and Substitution	
Signs of Operation	x
Product, Factor, Coefficient	x
Power	x
Algebraical Expression	x
Negative Quantities	x
Addition of Like Terms	x
Use of Brackets	x
Addition of Unlike Terms	x
Multiplication	
Simple Expressions or Monomials	x
Multiplication by a Negative Quantity	x
Rule of Signs	x
Commutative and Associate Laws	x
Law of Indices	x
Compound Expression	x
Distributive Law	x
Products by Inspection	x
Division	
Simple Expressions	x
Index Law	x
Compound Expressions	x
Brackets	
Removal of Brackets	x
Insertion of Brackets	x
Exercises for Review, Oral and Written	
Review of Elementary Rules	
Important Cases in Multiplication	x
Important Cases in Division	x
Formulæ and Their Use	
Simple Equations	
Use of Fundamental Axioms	x
Verification of Solutions	x
Transposition of Terms	x
Solving Problems using Simple Equations	
Symbolical Expression. Formulæ	
Easy Examples	x
Formation of Equations	x
Solving Problems using Equations	
Graphs	
Axes	x
Coordinates	x
Plotting Points	x

Note: Either introduction or Review with more difficult exercises worked

Appendix

Living Math Books 93
Choosing a Homeschool Math Curriculum or Textbook . . .95
Charlotte Mason's Math Timetables by Form 97
Variations on Scope and Sequence for Form I 98

Living Math Books

Ruby stood with her friend Donna, looking through the stacks at a used bookstore. Picking up a title, she remarked, "I saw this one on a 'Living Math Books' list online." Flipping through the picture book, she read aloud, "Count the bunnies looking fine, Marching in a bunny line." Putting the book down, Ruby remarked, "Hmm, that doesn't seem 'living.' "

"Not likely what Charlotte Mason had in mind," replied Donna. "Did you know Charlotte didn't even use what we think of as 'living math books' to teach math concepts? She felt mathematics is a speech in itself that is at once melodious and logical; therefore, mathematics is able to meet the requirements of the mind, and as such, it wasn't included in her rule of literary presentation."

"So we're left reading treatises to our children?" asked Ruby in surprise.

Donna laughed, "Not at all. I mean that using Charlotte's methods, mathematics are taught through the living speech of mathematics and not through books like *Five Flying Fairies*. I'm sure Charlotte's students ran into Archimedes in their reading of *Plutarch's Lives,* and we know short histories were used to excite interest in the different branches of mathematics. In fact, when my oldest was in high school he became interested in cryptography after reading Sarah Flannery's memoir, *In Code*. We would do well to use the guidelines Charlotte Mason gave us in choosing all our books, even those that include math concepts: Is it well-written? Does it put our child in touch with great ideas? . . ."

". . . Or is it childish twaddle?" finished Ruby, placing the picture book in her hands back in the stacks.

Charlotte Mason and Living Math Books

Charlotte Mason did not employ today's notion of "living math books" to teach or reinforce mathematical concepts. In fact, Charlotte believed that mathematics fell outside of her rule of literary presentation. Mathematics, Charlotte stated, is a speech in itself, both mellifluous and undeniably logical, and able to meet the requirements of mind.

Charlotte's students in grades 4–9 had only one book of literary presentation in their programme of mathematics study—a history of number told in story form that was to be read in their leisure time. That doesn't mean that our children cannot read exciting biographies about famous mathematicians to stimulate their interest in mathematics. It just means the modern lists of "living math books" look much different from Charlotte's.

"I have so far urged that knowledge is necessary to men, and that, in the initial stages, it must be conveyed through a literary medium, whether it be knowledge of physics or of Letters, because there would seem to be some inherent quality in mind which prepares it to respond to this form of appeal and no other. I say in the initial stages, because possibly, when the mind becomes conversant with knowledge of a given type, it unconsciously translates the driest formulae into living speech; perhaps it is for some such reason that mathematics seem to fall outside this rule

Notes

Irrefragibly *means "undeniably."*

of literary presentation; mathematics, like music, is a speech in itself, a speech irrefragibly logical, of exquisite clarity, meeting the requirements of mind" (Vol. 6, pp. 333, 334).

Books used by Charlotte's Students

Arithmetic

The ABC of Arithmetic by A. Sonnenschein and H. A. Nesbitt, M.A.
Pendlebury's New Concrete Arithmetic, Books I and V, by C. Pendlebury
A New Junior Arithmetic by Bompas Smith
Arithmetic for Children by A. E. A. Mair
The Science and Art of Arithmetic by A. Sonnenschein and H. A. Nesbitt
A New Shilling Arithmetic by C. Pendlebury
Longmans' Junior School Arithmetic

Geometry

Practical Exercises in Geometry by W. D. Eggar
Lessons in Experimental and Practical Geometry by H. S. Hall and F. H. Stevens
Inductive Geometry for Transition Classes by H. A. Nesbitt, M.A.
A First Step in Euclid by J. G. Bradshaw
Elements of Geometry by J. Hamblin Smith, M.A.

Algebra

A School Algebra by H. S. S. Hall

To Be Read in Leisure Time
(Grades 4 through 9)

Number Stories of Long Ago by David Eugene Smith

Suggested Reading for
Parents, Teachers, and Educators

The Teaching of Mathematics to Young Children by Irene Stephens
The Study of Arithmetic in Elementary Schools by A. Sonnenschein

Choosing a Homeschool Math Curriculum or Textbook

A look through Charlotte's programmes of study shows us that the PNEU took textbook choice seriously, seeking out those that best adhered to Charlotte's philosophy of education. The textbook was a tool, not the master, though; and a course was mapped out that best suited Charlotte's students, sometimes diverging from the given order, using common objects rather than prescribed, costly apparatus, supplementation with other materials, even altering a textbook's terminology at times. We also see that the PNEU was open to change when a math textbook came along which better fit Charlotte's methods for the teaching of mathematics or experience proved the textbook had too many disadvantages. Likewise, we can use Charlotte's guiding principles and methods to help us make wise choices when it comes to choosing textbooks or fine-tuning curriculum as we seek to make math an instrument for living teaching.

Look for a homeschool curriculum or textbook that will

- Provide for careful progression. We want a gradual unfolding of ideas, not simply a "getting through" of a course of study.
- Work well with a number of manipulatives in the introduction of concepts but not be shackled to them for the entire course of study.
- Not require expensive or complicated apparatus or work with only one type of manipulative. The child should be able to separate the facts from the objects used, so being able to utilize a variety of everyday objects is best.
- Not drown the subject in too much verbiage.
- Give examples that are interesting and aimed at reality; money sums and those involving the familiar are best.
- Give examples that, while interesting, are not too difficult.
- Give examples that work well with oral work. Children's work in Charlotte's classrooms was largely oral in the earlier years, and continuous oral practice was still given in later years.
- Assist the child in arriving at the method of solving problems or making discoveries himself.
- Facilitate reasoning powers not just mechanical ability.
- Allow for short lessons, no longer than 20 minutes in the earlier years and 30 minutes in the junior high or high school years.
- Allow you to adjust the pace for your child.
- Allow for mastery of concepts. Securing your child's understanding is a must before proceeding to the next concept.
- Allow for adequate review. Once a concept is mastered it will still need a sufficient review, and having examples of varying difficulty is best if your child progresses rapidly or for review the following term or year.

Notes

- Provide comprehensive explanations and answers in a teacher's guide if math is not (yet) your strong suit.

As your child advances in Arithmetic or into Practical Geometry, Formal Geometry, and Algebra and beyond, you will still want to use the above guidelines and look for textbooks or curriculum that will

- Guide the child in discovery and allow the child to think for oneself.
- Give exercises easily performed or easier types of equations in the introductory stage. This will facilitate accurate measurement and help secure neat and orderly arrangement while discovering or mastering rules.
- Begin with hands-on, experimental geometry before proceeding to a more formal study.
- Ensure a living treatment throughout. Practical exercises should continue along deductive exercises in geometry, and the practical side of algebra should be introduced as early as possible.
- Provide a slow, steady approach with lots of practice.
- Exclude long or tedious examples for calculation.
- Allow you to map out a course best suited for your child.

If you don't have a strong grasp of mathematics, please do not despair. Don't be surprised if, as you begin applying Charlotte's methods in mathematics, you also start seeing the reason behind the facts, discovering new relationships, and experiencing joy and delight while obtaining more mathematical understanding yourself. With the invaluable aid of a good curriculum and help from someone who can provide guidance when a concept cannot be grasped—or even if you are strong in mathematics or even a math teacher yourself—you can still be sure to

- Acquaint your child with those "captain" ideas Charlotte speaks of by introducing subjects or great thinkers through an interesting or exciting history.
- Insist upon neatness and accuracy from the very beginning and throughout.
- Have a good and respectful attitude toward mathematics and approach its study in a careful, thoughtful way.
- Be patient and advance slowly. Allow your child to wonder, discover, and permit ideas to germinate.
- Not over-teach or use too many words.
- Awaken a sense of awe in God's fixed laws of the universe.

Charlotte Mason's Math Timetables by Form

The charts below outline how Charlotte scheduled math classes and exercises for each grade level.

Grades 1-3	Monday	Tuesday	Wednesday	Thursday	Friday	Saturday	Number	IA	IB	Total
10:00-10:20	Number		Number		Number	Number	5 x 20 mins. 1 x 10 mins.	5 mins. exercise on tables daily	Rapid mental work	1 hr. 50 mins.
10:50-11:20		Number								
11:20-11:30				Number						

Grades 4-6	Monday	Tuesday	Wednesday	Thursday	Friday	Saturday	Arithmetic	Practical Geometry		Total
9:20-9:50	Arithmetic	Arithmetic	Arithmetic	Arithmetic	Arithmetic (Practical Geometry)	Arithmetic	2 hrs. per week includes 5 mins. mental math	30 mins. per week		2 hrs. 30 mins.

Grades 7-8	Monday	Tuesday	Wednesday	Thursday	Friday	Saturday	Arithmetic	Mental Arithmetic	Euclid	Total
9:20-9:50	Arithmetic		Arithmetic		Euclid	Arithmetic	3 x 30 mins. lessons	3x 10 mins. sessions	30 mins. per week 10 mins. repetition	2 hrs. 50 mins.
10:50-11:00			Repetition: Euclid							
11:20-11:30	Arithmetic (Mental)	Arithmetic (Mental)		Arithmetic (Mental)		Euclid				

Grade 9	Monday	Tuesday	Wednesday	Thursday	Friday	Saturday	Arithmetic	Euclid	Algebra	Total
9:30-10:00	Arithmetic	Euclid		Arithmetic	Euclid	Algebra	2 x 30 mins.	2 x 30 mins.	2 x 30 mins.	3 hrs.
11:45-12:15		Algebra								

Grades 10-12	Monday	Tuesday	Wednesday	Thursday	Friday	Saturday	Arithmetic	Euclid	Algebra	Total
9:00-9:30	Arithmetic		Algebra			Algebra	2 x 30 mins.	2 x 30 mins.	2 x 30 mins.	3 hrs.
9:300-10:00	Arithmetic	Euclid		Arithmetic	Euclid					

Appendix

Variations on Scope and Sequence for Form I

(Note: Stephens' scope and sequence was used as the basis for the Arithmetic chart on pages 46–48.)

Programmes 42-44 (13 years since the PRS began)			
	Form I		
	IB	IA	
Approximate U.S. Grade	1	2	3
Approximate U.S. Age	6-7	7-8	8-9
Analysis of Numbers *			
One to ten.	x		
Eleven and Twelve.	x		
Thirteen to Twenty.	x		
Twenty to One Hundred.	x		
Counting up to One Hundred.	x		
Analysis of Numbers Under One Hundred.	x		
Addition of Pairs of Numbers.	x		
Analysis of Numbers under Two Hundred.	x		
Analysis of Numbers Under a Thousand		x	x
Money Questions		x	x
Addition		x	x
Subtraction		x	x
Multiplication Tables up to 6x12		x	
Multiplication Tables up to 12x12			x

* i.e., investigation of each number by working out addition and subtraction sums involving its use. Initially done with the aid of manipulatives then proceeding to oral work with the writing of sums used very sparingly.

Programmes 90-94 (30 years since the PRS began)			
	Form I		
	IB	IA	
Approximate U.S. Grade	1	2	3
Approximate U.S. Age	6-7	7-8	8-9
Decomposition of Numbers *			
Decomposing numbers as far as 24.	x		
Money sums as far as 25 cents.	x		
Work with measurements up to 2 feet (24 inches).	x		
Work with weight measurements up to 1½ lb. (24 ounces).	x		
Multiplication - Proof of two times and other tables as far as 24 by means of practical exercises.	x		
Rapid mental work.	x		
Addition, Subtraction, Multiplication and Division of numbers as far as 60.	x		
Money exercises to 50 cents.	x		
Measuring practice up to 5 ft. (60 inches).	x		
Weighing practice to 20 lb.	x		
Shopping exercises in weights and values up to 20 lb. and up to 50 cents.	x		
Rapid mental work.	x		
The four rules with number problems as far as 100.	x		
Proofs and tables up to 100.	x		
Work with measurements up to 6 feet.	x		
Work with weight measurements up to 28 lbs.	x		
Shopping exercises worked up to $1.00.	x		
Rapid mental work.	x		
Review of previous year's work.		x	x
Exercises in addition and subtraction.		x	x
Multiplication and division of numbers to 250 by numbers up to 12.		x	
Prime factors of numbers up to 20.		x	
Proof of tables to 12 times.		x	
Number of inches in a square foot.		x	
Measuring. - Exercises in length up to 12 ft.		x	
Weighing. - Exercises in ounces and pounds up to 28 pounds.		x	
Exercises in amounts up to $1.25.		x	
Tables up to 12x12 (five minutes' exercise in every lesson to be worked out in money).		x	x
Multiplication and Division of numbers to 1,000 by numbers up to 12.			x
Prime factors of numbers up to 72.			x
Practical work with simple fractions and simple decimals.			x
Measuring. - Exercises in the four rules with lengths as far as 15 ft.; weights as far as 28 lb.; liquid measures as far as a gallon.			x
Exercises with amounts up to $10.00.			x
Time. - Reading of clocks and watches and the calendar.			x

* i.e., breaking a whole number into two parts or working with different combinations of numbers to obtain the whole, e.g., 1+5=6, 2+4=6, 3+3=6.

Appendix

Programmes 90-94 using a different textbook	Form I		
	IB	IA	
Approximate U.S. Grade	1	2	3
Approximate U.S. Age	6-7	7-8	8-9
Decomposition of Numbers *			
Decomposing numbers as far as 24.	x		
Money sums as far as 25 cents.	x		
Work with measurements up to 2 feet (24 inches).	x		
Work with weight measurements up to 1½ lb. (24 ounces).	x		
Multiplication - Proof of two times and other tables as far as 24 by means of practical exercises.	x		
Rapid mental work.	x		
Addition, Subtraction, Multiplication and Division of numbers as far as 60.	x		
Money exercises to 50 cents.	x		
Measuring practice up to 5 ft. (60 inches).	x		
Weighing practice to 20 lb.	x		
Shopping exercies in weights and values up to 20 lb. and up to 50 cents.	x		
Rapid mental work.	x		
The four rules with number problems as far as 100.	x		
Proofs and tables up to 100.	x		
Work with measurements up to 6 feet.	x		
Work with weight measurements up to 28 lbs.	x		
Shopping exercises worked up to $1.00.	x		
Rapid mental work.	x		
Addition rules.		x	
Count by twos, from 1 to 100.		x	
Count by threes, fours, etc., up to twelves, from 1 to 100.		x	
Addition with up to five sets of figures.		x	
Add numbers within 1,000.		x	
Add numbers within 10,000.			x
Subtract numbers within 1,000.		x	
Subtract numbers within 10,000.			x
Addition and Subtraction using brackets.		x	x
Reduction of money ie., converting a quantity from one denomination to another (either a higher or lower denomination).		x	x
Harder compound addition and subtraction.			x
Multiplication with numbers within 1,000.		x	
Multiplication with numbers within 10,000.			x
Tables up to 12x12.			x
Areas - Finding Square Inches and Square Feet			x
Short Division.		x	
Short Division of Money		x	
Measures of time.		x	x
Fractions ½, ¼, ⅓, and ⅛.			x
Weights and Measures.			

* i.e., breaking a whole number into two parts or working with different combinations of numbers to obtain the whole, e.g., 1+5=6, 2+4=6, 3+3=6.

The Teaching of Mathematics to Young Children by Irene Stephens 1911	Form I		
	IB	IA	
Approximate U.S. Grade	1	2	3
Approximate U.S. Age	6-7	7-8	8-9
Analysis of Numbers *			
One through Nine.	x		
Meanings of Symbols.	x		
Notation	x		
The Number 10	x		
Units, Ten Bundles	x		
Eleven through Twenty	x		
Idea of Place Value	x		
Introduction of Money.	x		
Reduction of Money.	x		
Simple Money Sums	x		
Twenty through Thirty	x		
30-100 (taken in groups of ten)	x		
Understand numeration and notation up to 1000.		x	
Understand numeration and notation up to 10,000.			x
The Four Rules and Tables			
Addition			
Review previous years' work.		x	x
Understand the idea of addition.		x	
Money sums in addition.		x	x
Sums on pure number.		x	x
Longer sums with three or four sets of figures.		x	
Add numbers within 1000.		x	
Add numbers within 10,000.			x
Harder compound addition			x
Subtraction			
Review previous years' work.		x	x
Understand the idea of subtraction.		x	
Money sums.		x	x
Pure number subtraction sums.		x	x
Subtract numbers within 1000.		x	
Subtract numbers within 10,000.			x
Harder compound subtraction			x
Multiplication			
Review previous years' work.		x	x
Present as extension to addition by using repeated addition to solve problems.			
Simple Multiplication to show the idea of "times."		x	
Introduce the symbol "x"		x	
Construction of multiplication tables by student.		x	x
Master multiplication table up to 6x12.		x	
Master multiplication table up to 12x12.			x
Multiplication problems involving money.		x	x
Pure number multiplication with problems involving real things.		x	x
Multiplication by 10's, 100's, 1000's.		x	
Division			
Review previous years' work.		x	x
The idea of division as continuous subtraction through sharing and grouping exercises worked with manipulatives.		x	
Introduce the symbol "÷"		x	
Simple money sums involving division.		x	
Short division.		x	
Long division introduced.			x
Simple fractions introduced.			x

* i.e., investigation of each number by working out addition and subtraction sums involving its use. Initially done with the aid of manipulatives then proceeding to oral work with the writing of sums used very sparingly.